BUILDING
an
Intentional
School
Culture

To my sons,
Jason
&
David,
with love
C. E.

To my parents, Betty and Kerwin,
for their love and for their commitment
to education
D. F.

BUILDING
an
Intentional
School
Culture

EXCELLENCE in ACADEMICS and CHARACTER

CHARLES F. ELBOT ◆ **DAVID FULTON**

CORWIN PRESS
A SAGE Publications Company
Thousand Oaks, CA 91320

For information:

Corwin Press
A Sage Publications Company
2455 Teller Road
Thousand Oaks, California 91320
www.corwinpress.com

Sage Publications Ltd.
1 Oliver's Yard
55 City Road
London EC1Y 1SP
United Kingdom

Sage Publications India Pvt. Ltd.
B 1/I 1 Mohan Cooperative
   Industrial Area
Mathura Road, New Delhi 110 044
India

Sage Publications Asia-Pacific Pte. Ltd.
33 Pekin Street #02-01
Far East Square
Singapore 048763

Library of Congress Cataloging-in-Publication Data

Elbot, Charles F.
Building an intentional school culture: Excellence in academics and character/
Charles F. Elbot, David Fulton.
      p. cm.
Includes bibliographical references and index.
ISBN 978-1-4129-5377-1 (cloth)
ISBN 978-1-4129-5378-8 (pbk.)
   1. School improvement programs. 2. School environment
I. Fulton, David, PhD II. Title.

LB2822.8E38 2008
371.2—dc22   2007020186

This book is printed on acid-free paper.

07   08   09   10   11   10 9 8 7 6 5 4 3 2 1

Acquisitions Editor:	Elizabeth Brenkus
Editorial Assistants:	Desirée Enayati and Ena Rosen
Project Editor:	Astrid Virding
Copy Editor:	Jovey Stewart
Typesetter:	C&M Digitals (P) Ltd.
Proofreader:	Dennis Webb
Indexer:	Juniee Oneida
Cover Designer:	Michael Dubowe

Contents

Preface

By 2002, Charles Elbot had served as a school principal in public and independent schools for 20 years, when he approached the superintendent of the Denver Public Schools about the need to more intentionally educate students for character, since the goal of education should include not only the mastery of knowledge and skills but also the development of character and the mastery of self. At the same time, David Fulton was defending his doctoral dissertation, "Forgiveness and Education," at the University of Wisconsin, Madison, and was heading to Northern Ireland to work with schools as part of the International Forgiveness Institute.

The superintendent gave his blessing for Charles to begin character education work if he could find outside funding, which—thanks to local foundations and the federal government—he was able to do. Shortly thereafter, David Fulton joined the team, as did Barb Evans as administrative assistant. These three began working with 30 schools based largely on strategies Charles had developed as a school leader. Their work expanded to more than 60 schools and included service learning, student leadership development, and civic engagement.

It soon became clear that they (we) were actually involved in much more than the narrow work of character education, which invariably is seen as simply "one more thing." Instead of only helping schools identify and promote core values, we began helping each school build a culture that created coherence among all elements of school life. We were not adding one more item to a school's plate but were helping each school shape the plate itself. It is interesting that few schools are skilled at systematically crafting their school culture to enhance student learning. Just as the recent emphasis on assessment and school accountability has proven to be an important resource for school improvement, we feel that the harnessing of school culture is of great consequence as well.

In this book, we share what we have learned from working with these schools over the past four years. We share the strategies and tools we have used to assess and shape school culture and include many stories— sometimes composites of stories—from our work with schools. In our research, we found a dearth of books and materials on school culture that bridged the gap between theory and the practice, and we hope this book helps address this need. This book is for school leaders, teachers, policy-makers, parents, and anyone interested in improving the way schools work. In an era of tight funding, schools must find ways to do more with fewer resources: we feel that harnessing your school culture is one such way.

Plato's three ways of knowing offers a helpful perspective on school culture in the education of young people. Plato described the first way of knowing as the *True*. The *True* is what most of our academic standards focus on: academic content and skills. But knowing facts is clearly not enough. Some schools are very successful at teaching literacy and math but fail to go beyond the *True* and connect knowledge to the everyday fabric of our lives. We have all heard the stories of highly educated scientists building efficient gas chambers in Nazi Germany. So should education stop at being "smart?"

The second way of knowing is the *Good*. This is about being virtuous: about not only identifying with "me" but also with "we." It is about empathy, service to others, good citizenship, and character education. This is the realm where the richness of literature, history, science, and other content areas inform our daily interactions.

The third way of knowing is the *Beautiful*, which is about spirit, presence, poetry, and artistic sensibility. Here, learning goes beyond information and practical application to exploring the possibilities of being a human being. A school culture can be designed deliberately to hold each of these three ways of knowing and foster ways for all three to resonate with each other so our young people can build flourishing lives, contribute to their communities, and be of benefit to the generations who follow them.

On page xiv is a diagram reflecting key components of this book, which align with the book's chapters. In the middle circle are a head, a hand, and a heart, which correspond to the True, the Good, and the Beautiful. These make up the whole student, the whole person. Encircling the student is the touchstone, which is a school creed containing a set of universal principles. When integrated into the school culture, it guides the growth of students. The next layer of the diagram describes four mindsets—dependence, independence, interdependence, and integration—which are mental models for interacting with the world. The goal is for a school to shift its members toward more integrated ways of thinking and acting which enhances everyone's life.

The eight gateways represent distinct entry points for shaping a school culture, which is useful because it is impossible to shape all aspects of your culture at once. The gateways include the quality of relationships; student voice; the physical environment; and expectations, trust, and accountability.

Adaptations from other cultures comprise the outer layer of the diagram. It is as much a suggested orientation as it is a tool. Although we give examples of how schools can learn from corporate culture, medical culture, and ethnic cultures, we leave this area open for further exploration. A school that is developing a particular aspect of its culture would do well to research the richness of insights from other cultures.

Drawing on research on school culture and on our experience from working with dozens of schools, we developed these four tools, a variety of instruments, and blueprints to assist schools. We expect that each school, with its unique strengths and challenges, will use these tools in its own particular manner. But just as building a house follows certain logic—foundation, then walls, then roof—we feel that building a culture does as well. We therefore present a suggested sequence for using these tools in Chapter 5, "Applying the Four Tools."

This is clearly a work in progress, and we do not pretend to have found all the answers to create the perfect school. As we deepen our work with schools, we are presented with even more questions: Why does a faculty that is highly *independent* in its thinking and professional work tend to keep their students in *dependent* roles while teachers who think and work out of a mind-set of *interdependence* readily foster student *independent* and *interdependent* thinking and behavior? What are the implications of teacher mind-sets on the education of our young people?

It is our sincere hope that after reading this book you will look at your school as full of possibilities and then approach the shaping of its culture in a way that promotes academic achievement and enhances the well-being of your students and teachers alike.

Acknowledgments

We have many people to thank for making this work possible. They include the site-coordinators, teachers, and principals of our schools. Thanks are due to Nicole Tembrock, who joined our team a year ago and has made many contributions to our work. Special thanks also go to Barb Evans, who did all of the graphics for this book. This book could not have been written without the many broad shoulders of thoughtful writers and educators upon which we stand.

Corwin Press gratefully acknowledges the contributions of the following individuals:

Jennifer Baadsgaard, Assistant Principal
Roosevelt High School
San Antonio, Texas

Launa Ellison, Fifth- and Sixth-Grade Teacher, Consultant, and Author
Clara Barton School
Minneapolis, Minnesota

About the Authors

**Charles F. Elbot** was born in Europe and lived his first 20 years as part of three cultures—French, German, and American. After graduating from Wesleyan University, he pursued his dream to see the world. With his backpack, sleeping bag, and only a few hundred dollars, he traveled west, crossing Asia, Africa, the Middle East, and Europe over a three-year period. For funds, he worked on ships out of Bali and Singapore. These were three extraordinary years of being exposed to a rich array of the world's cultures.

Upon returning to the United States, he began teaching and then helped to found an alternative high school, September School, in Boulder, Colorado. After several years of teaching and serving as a principal, he attended Harvard University, earning his master's degree in moral development and educational administration. Over the next 21 years, he served as a principal in public and independent schools.

Charles served as principal of Slavens School, a K–8 Denver public school, which in 2001 was honored as one of eight schools in the nation as a National School of Character. This school also was recognized for its extraordinary student academic achievement. These accomplishments attracted educators from around the country who spent days observing "how" things were done at the school. The following year Charles founded the Office of Character and School Culture and began to take these ideas to other schools in Denver and around the country. In 2003, the New Zealand government invited Charles to share these approaches with educators in New Zealand. Since then, the Office of Character and School Culture has continued to develop the work of harnessing a school's culture to build excellence in academics and character, culminating in this book.

Charles is married to Barbara Robertson Elbot, and they have two children, Jason and David.

 **David Fulton**—After graduating from Emory University, David Fulton taught high school and middle school for four years in Denver, Colorado. While in graduate school, he worked for the State Department of Education in Wisconsin, was a researcher for a National Science Foundation–funded school reform project, and supervised preservice social studies teachers. After completing his master's and PhD from the University of Wisconsin–Madison in foundations of education, he lived in Northern Ireland as part of the International Forgiveness Institute. In 2003, he joined the Denver Public Schools Office of Character and School Culture. He is an adjunct faculty member at the University of Denver–School of Education and has taught courses at the University of Colorado–Boulder and at the University of Wisconsin–Madison.

Traditional School Culture
Student Achievement

Principal → Faculty/Staff → Students → **Student Achievement**

Parents → Students

Intentional School Culture
Student Achievement

Principal
(Leadership)

Parents
(Partnership)

Faculty/Staff
(Collaboration)

Students
(Engagement)

Student Achievement

THE INTENTIONAL SCHOOL CULTURE

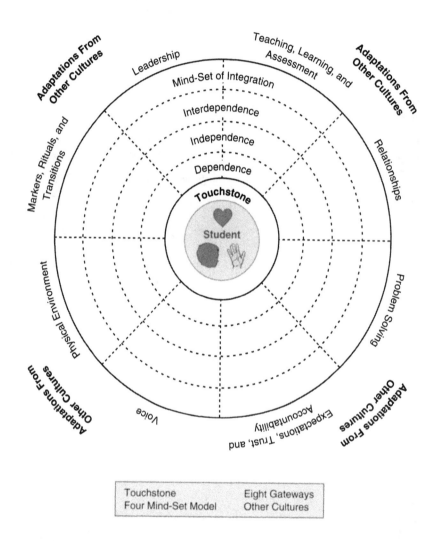

Touchstone	Eight Gateways
Four Mind-Set Model	Other Cultures

"This has proven to be the most remarkable work we have committed ourselves to at our school. Our children made a mid-year shift showing less aggression and more cooperation. Our discipline made a similar shift from punitive to restorative. We are growing, learning, and trying new things, and I feel that it will only get better here. Teachers have commented on the change, and our newfound perspective on teaching, that words like love, compassion, honesty, kindness, and integrity have become a part of our daily vocabulary."

—Denver public school teacher

1

Building an Intentional School Culture

Excellence in Academics and Character

To anyone who takes a close look at what goes on in classrooms it becomes quickly evident that our schools do much more than pass along requisite knowledge to the students attending them (or fail to do so, as the case may be). They also influence the way those students look upon themselves and others. They affect the way learning is valued and sought after and lay the foundations of lifelong habits of thought and action. They shape opinion and develop taste, helping to form liking and aversions. They contribute to the growth of character and, in some instances they may even be a factor in its corruption. Schools in aggregate do all this and more to and for the students they serve. Moreover and here is the important point, they do much of it without the full awareness and thoughtful engagement of those in charge.

—William Jackson, Robert Boostrom, and
David Hansen, *The Moral Life of Schools* (1993)

This book is about school culture: what it is and how to shape it. We make two central and related arguments: first, that a school's culture has a significant impact on the lives of students, including on their character and academic development, and second, that the four tools we present can help a school both understand and deliberately shape its culture.

To consistently build excellence for students, families, and for the community, a school must have an intentional culture based on shared values, beliefs, and behaviors. As educators, we tend to focus on improving our school's curriculum, teacher training, and school leadership. Though we have made significant gains in these areas, we must look at the untapped potential of building an intentional school culture, for it is the school culture that serves as the medium for growing our students and teachers.

"It is difficult to foresee what the schools of the new millennium will look like. Many of our schools seem en route to becoming a hybrid of a nineteenth-century factory, a twentieth-century minimum security penal colony, and a twenty-first-century Educational Testing Service. I prefer a different future. If you want to predict the future, create it! This is precisely what school people now have the opportunity—the imperative—to do. . . . There is no more important work."
—Roland Barth, Harvard University professor (2001), p. 213

A school's culture—whether vibrant, adaptive, and thriving, or toxic and dying—affects everything associated with the school. Many educators do not intentionally shape their school's culture because they feel that they lack the tools to do so. A school culture therefore tends to haphazardly unfold, sometimes in response to parental pressure, a principal's personality, and/or educational fads. This is true even at new schools, where staff members may pay attention to the design of both the building and the curriculum, but fail to design for an effective school culture.

The graphic organizer presented previous to page 1 shows the relationship between the four tools for shaping school culture: the school touchstone, the Four Mind-Set Model, the eight gateways, and lessons from fields outside of education. The bulk of this book is dedicated to exploring these four tools, which ultimately cultivate a student's intellect (head), competence (hand), and compassion (heart).

The school touchstone is a short statement that expresses the core qualities—both academic and ethical—that a school community seeks to develop in its members, and it serves as a guide for daily thinking and action. The Four Mind-Set Model depicts four different mind-sets—dependence, independence, interdependence, and integration—for approaching the work of schooling. The eight gateways represent eight entry points for shaping a school culture; they include teaching and learning, student voice, and the physical environment of the school. Finally, knowledge of how organizations and fields outside of education have shaped their cultures can inform the shaping of a school's culture. Taken as a whole, we believe that this work provides insights for both understanding and deliberately shaping school culture. A poster in one of our schools reads, "If the educators don't take the lead in shaping their school's culture, then other forces will." Given the impact that a school's culture can have on a student's life—both present and future—the stakes are simply too high to leave its shaping to chance: adults need to thoughtfully and deliberately create the kind of educational environment in which every student can flourish. Paul Houston and Stephen Sokolow (2006) write in *The Spiritual Dimension of Leadership*:

"Community is the tie that binds students and teachers together in special ways, to something more significant than themselves: shared values and ideals. It lifts both teachers and students to higher levels of self-understanding, commitment and performance . . . thus providing them with a unique and enduring sense of identity, belonging and place."
—*Thomas Sergiovanni, author (1994)*

Whether [or not] you realize it, your intentions set up an energy field around themselves. You strengthen that field by what you think and what you envision. You strengthen it by what you write and what you say and by enrolling people through collaborative processes. The more explicit you make your intentions and the more time and energy you give to implementing them, the more you increase the likelihood of seeing your intentions actually manifest in reality. Intention is not only a principle: It is a power, a force. (p. 2)

The Importance of School Culture

On one level, few would question that a school's culture has a strong impact on both the students and the adults. As Harvard professor Roland Barth suggests, its influence is undeniable: "A school's culture has far more influence on life and learning in the schoolhouse than the state department of education, the superintendent, the school board, or even the principal can ever have" (Barth, 2002, p. 7). However, few educators seem to appreciate just how important culture is and actually take steps to intentionally shape it. There is now a growing set of data supporting the importance of this kind of work.

Michael Fullan (2005) notes that of the 134 secondary schools in England that were part of the 2004 Hay Group study, the "successful schools had a much more demanding culture—hunger for improvement, promoting excellence, holding hope for every child—while the less successful schools had less of a press on improvement and were more forgiving if results were not forthcoming" (p. 58).

In *Trust in Schools: A Core Resource for Improvement*, Anthony Bryk and Barbara Schneider (2002) make the case, empirically, that the top academically performing schools in their study of Chicago public schools also score high on a measure they call "relational trust." This concept relates to how well each key stakeholder in a school community—students, parents, teachers, and administration—believes that members of the other groups are fulfilling their role obligations. It is also a strong proxy for the quality of relationships within a school, a central aspect of school culture.

> *"When a school has a positive, professional culture, one finds meaningful staff development, successful curricular reform, and the effective use of student performance data. In these cultures, staff and student learning thrive. In contrast, a school with a negative or toxic culture that does not value professional learning, resists change, or devalues staff development hinders success. School culture will have either a positive or a detrimental impact on the quality and success of staff development."*
>
> *—Kent Petersen, author (2002), p. 10*

Perhaps more important, Bryk and Schneider also demonstrate that high relational trust is predictive of academic success. In other words, schools with improving relational trust also tend to see improving test scores. On the other hand, the authors found that schools with persistently low trust had "virtually no chance of showing improvement" in either reading or mathematics (Bryk & Schneider, 2002).

In *Improving School Climate and Culture,* Gonder and Hymes (1994) noted that the research has found a strong link between a positive school climate and high staff productivity and student achievement. In fact, a review of the research on the effect of school climate on student achievement shows that climate or culture has a great influence on a student's chance for success. Furthermore, a Kentucky study of twenty schools on the relationship of school climate to the implementation of school reform found that school climate was a significant factor in implementing successful school reform (Bulach & Malone, 1994).

Similarly, after looking at longitudinal data on school reform, researchers from the Center on Organization and Restructuring of Schools at the University of Wisconsin–Madison noted that the importance of school relations is often overlooked:

> Our research suggests that human resources—such as openness to improvement, trust and respect, teachers having knowledge and skills, supportive leadership and socialization—are more critical to the development of professional communities than structural conditions. . . . [T]he need to improve the culture, climate and interpersonal relationships in schools have [sic] received too little attention. (Byrk, A., & Schneider, B., 2002, p. 8; Reprinted with permission)

Laneer Middle School: The Shaping of a School Culture

In what follows, we present a picture of what deliberately shaping a school culture might look like. The story of Laneer Middle School is a composite, based on our experiences at numerous schools. In the narrative, you will be introduced to the major tools the school staff and administrators used in the process. Throughout the rest of the book, we explore in much greater depth both the nature of those tools and how to use them.

Laneer Middle School is considered a good school. Its state test scores have risen over the past five years, partly a result of the many new efforts by the staff and principal. They implemented the new district literacy and math programs and hired math and literacy coaches. The school formed faculty study groups that focus on using student assessment data to drive instruction and purchased software to provide disaggregated feedback on student performance. The administration has attended numerous conferences to learn more about instruction and assessment. All these efforts have paid off.

However, the school's scores had plateaued during the past two years. The staff had become frustrated, believing they simply couldn't work any harder at what they were presently doing. They were maxed out. After reviewing the many changes they had made, the staff realized there was one fundamental aspect of their school they hadn't fully explored: creating an intentional culture. Their efforts to align teaching and assessments defined part of their culture, but what if they could align all aspects of their school culture toward a common goal? The principal contacted the Office of Character and School Culture for assistance.

Laneer's principal met with Jeanine Mains, a former school principal, in a small office on the third floor of the administration building where Jeanine shared recent literature and data linking school culture to school improvement. The principal asked, "The culture of Laneer includes everything. How do you work with everything?" Jeanine reassured her that there was a road map to approach this work in stages, and she described the four tools that can be used to intentionally shape the culture of Laneer. What follows is a brief account of a two-year journey toward shaping an intentional school culture. It does not, of course, reflect the many bumps along the way, but it does illustrate the steps in the process of building a school culture.

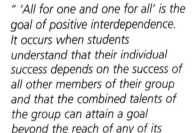

" 'All for one and one for all' is the goal of positive interdependence. It occurs when students understand that their individual success depends on the success of all other members of their group and that the combined talents of the group can attain a goal beyond the reach of any of its separate members."
—Performance Learning Systems, Cooperative Learning (2004)

The staff of Laneer read and discussed background information on school culture, met with Jeanine to ask her questions, reached consensus to take on this work, and then formed a committee to move it forward. The committee began a deep analysis of their current school culture. They reviewed past school satisfaction surveys from students, staff, and parents to discern perceived strengths and weaknesses. Jeanine asked the staff to respond to the School Culture Survey (10 minutes) and the Eight Gateway Survey (30 minutes). Some teachers elicited student, parent, and staff input by inviting them to respond on posters to the following questions: "What I want to preserve at Laneer Middle School" and "What I want to change." The student council also interviewed students regarding their experiences at Laneer. They asked questions such as, "What is the most powerful tradition for you at LMS?" and "How many adults do you think care about you?" Some of the responses were surprising. After two months of compiling and synthesizing data, the School Culture Committee identified the following patterns, mind-sets, and weakest links at Laneer Middle School.

1. Faculty members are highly independent in how they function at school; their lowest scores on the Rubric for Faculty Interdependence were in the areas of speech, trust, psychological safety, and collaborative decision making.

2. Faculty members make an unspoken attempt to keep students in highly dependent roles because most teachers believe that it is easier to control students when they are not given too much independent responsibility.

3. The majority of parents were more involved with their child's elementary school than with Laneer. Here, they drop their child off at school and assume (or hope) that the school will educate their child. A few parents are overly involved with their child's education by demanding specific teachers, rescuing their child from having to take responsibility for his or her behavior, and by regularly insisting on project time extensions. Some parents have figured out healthy and effective ways to partner with their child's middle school.

4. At Laneer, as at most schools, "time on task" is the constant and "learning" is the big variable. For instance, some students need more time to understand algebraic thinking while other students need less. In reviewing its culture, the staff began to ask how mastery learning could become more of the constant and time the variable.

5. Students noted the bare walls. Their elementary schools' walls had been covered with student work and interesting educational displays.

6. The Eight Gateways Survey revealed the following insights: teachers have a wide range of academic and behavioral expectations of students; much of the problem solving does not get to root causes; students have almost no voice in the school; the school's explicit traditions are wanting, while student-created traditions of hazing and bullying are prevalent; and the principal is in a double-bind because the staff wants her to take care of issues, yet the staff wants to have a voice in what and how things are done.

7. The most widely agreed-on concern was that although the school had a mission and vision statement, "how" things were done varied enormously throughout the school. For example, teachers, students, and parents had virtually no shared agreement about homework. Some teachers believe that homework reinforces academic knowledge and teaches important skills

such as time management, whereas other teachers feel that assigning homework is a waste of time. As a result, many students do their homework in a perfunctory manner and turn in very low quality work. Similarly, the staff is not on the same page regarding student behavior. One teacher ignored an eighth grader who punched another kid in history class, even though it happened right in front of him. Yet when a seventh grader pushed a kid into a locker, he was suspended for two days by the assistant principal. This lack of shared norms is an enormous source of conflict for the whole school community.

The faculty reviewed this information and met with Jeanine to develop a school touchstone to define how things are to be done at Laneer. After looking at touchstones from other schools and other organizations, such as Toyota, the staff agreed to the following set of priority values.

The Laneer Touchstone

At Laneer Middle School we take the high road.
We weave the vitality, caring, and intelligence of students,
parents, and teachers to excel in scholarship and character.
We deal with the root causes of our issues by engaging in
courageous conversations. We have a stake in the well-being of
others and give our best in and out of the classroom.
This is who we are even when no one is watching!

The draft of this touchstone was shared with students, parents, and staff. After it was finalized, the school held an assembly where the students and staff discussed the use of the touchstone in daily life and were then invited to sign the large touchstone banner. This powerful ceremony included student and teacher speakers who shared personal life stories associated with the touchstone qualities. Shortly thereafter, the school promoted the Laneer touchstone in many creative ways, including classroom posters, student ID cards, refrigerator magnets for parents, newsletters, and morning announcements.

Teachers connected the touchstone qualities to their subject content. The seventh-grade history course, for example, highlights the courageous conversations of our founding fathers that led to the Declaration of Independence. The science teacher refers to how most scientific discoveries today are team efforts and underscores the importance of tapping into the vitality, caring, and intelligence of the group. The School Culture Committee developed rubrics for each of the touchstone qualities. These rubrics were used to enhance the self-awareness of students and have helped guide discussions between teachers and students.

Eventually, the Laneer touchstone guided all school activities, including after-school clubs and programs, field trips, and parent-teacher interactions. These shared school norms of "how we do things" at Laneer Middle

School fundamentally altered the old school culture. Now everyone at Laneer is stretched to speak and act in more thoughtful, responsible, and caring ways. Although this work took some effort, the school has benefited from students, staff, and parents working out of a purposeful and shared school culture.

"Teachers who have worked together see substantial improvements in student achievement, behavior, and attitude. Teachers in a junior high school traced their students' remarkable gains in math achievement and the virtual elimination of classroom behavior problems to the revisions in curriculum, testing, and placement procedures they had achieved working as a group. In schools where teachers work collaboratively, students can sense the program coherence and a consistency of expectations, which may explain the improved behavior and achievement."

—Morton Inger, author (1993)

The staff chose to develop specific shared agreements for themselves on such areas as a commitment to teamwork and created rubrics for each agreement. They began with self-assessments, but once trust was built, they engaged in peer reflections. Twice a year, the staff—including the principal and the custodians—provided anonymous feedback on how well each person was upholding the shared agreements. (Only the individual saw his or her results.) This feedback has helped create more consistency among the staff.

As the use of the touchstone organically grew throughout the school community, the faculty began a systematic review of how each of the three partners (faculty and staff, students, and parents) could think and act in more highly integrated ways, as presented by the Four Mind-Set Model. Because teachers functioned in primarily independent ways, the faculty discussed ways in which they could collaborate. They then discussed how to cultivate more independent and interdependent student responsibility. One teacher shared how those parents who worked out of the interdependence paradigm created all sorts of teaching and learning possibilities for her seventh-grade art students. She also shared her desire for more parents to act interdependently, asking "Wouldn't it be neat if all parents asked not what Laneer Middle School could do for them, but asked what they could do for LMS?"

The faculty decided to focus on increasing student ownership of their learning. Too many students sat passively in classes waiting to be "filled" by their teachers (dependence). Since most teachers approached students from an authoritarian position, teachers looked at other models of teaching, such as cooperative learning, coaching, and service learning. After much discussion, they reached some general agreements on the kinds of situations in which students of each grade level (sixth, seventh, and eighth) would have little input, situations that were open to negotiation, and areas over which students could independently make decisions.

Teachers also provided guidelines for parental involvement with homework. These guidelines reaffirmed that homework was the job of students, not parents. Parents can help promote good study habits, but students should be the ones doing the work, as well as remembering to take the necessary materials home and then back to school. Students must manage their time and learn how to schedule their evenings so they can complete their assignments. They must also develop a sense of what high-quality work looks like. Each school year, parents should become less involved with their child's homework.

As the first year of creating an intentional school culture came to a close, the school reviewed what it had accomplished and looked to the next year. There was general agreement that an in-depth look at their school culture had revealed many hidden beliefs and practices that kept them from fulfilling the school's mission, vision, and goals. Everyone agreed that having a shared school touchstone was providing alignment and coherence for how things were being done. Teachers enjoyed using curricular content to reinforce parts of the touchstone.

However, two staff reflections, based on shared agreements, proved to be more controversial. After exploring individual concerns, the staff reached a consensus to continue with this practice (of staff reflections) even though it created a certain amount of discomfort. For instance, it had been hard for the principal to deal with the feedback that she had been less than respectful in some of her interactions with staff. She learned that on numerous occasions she had cut someone off in mid sentence by a curt response. Everyone agreed that the agreements and the feedback process created a powerful means of uplifting adult behavior, which also made the staff better role models for students.

Teachers also felt that their shared intention to cultivate greater student independence and interdependence had enormous potential. A seventh-grade teacher stated that when she had given her students additional freedom on their projects, she had been pleasantly surprised by the results. She proclaimed, "When I started to trust my students more, and gave them more responsibility—as well as held them accountable—they did amazing work."

Based on this success, the faculty decided to explore how using the eight gateways the next school year could encourage even more students to take responsibility for their learning.

The first gateway the faculty explored was the physical environment of the school. How could it be shaped to encourage more independent student thinking and acting? The faculty decided to designate an outside deck as a place where eighth graders could hang out and even eat lunch together. It would be considered their own special space. The eighth graders, however, had to behave responsibly. Leaving trash, fighting, or otherwise behaving inappropriately would be grounds for losing this privilege. The staff felt that this independence and increased responsibility would be good preparation for high school.

Each of the three grades was given a hallway bulletin board for grade-level student communication. The school also could add three minutes to the end of the school day during which all students and staff picked up trash, organized lockers, and left the facilities as clean and tidy as when they found them at the beginning of the day.

Teachers exhibited student work and created opportunities for student voice in novel ways. Student council meetings were videotaped and run the next day on several hallway monitors. Student art work, student writing, various projects, and elegant solutions to math problems were displayed for all to review. In these and other ways, the staff (and students) deliberately shaped the physical environment to encourage more student ownership in their own learning. This led to more pride and, eventually, higher-quality work.

In a similar manner, the school explored how each of the other seven gateways could contribute to moving students from dependent mind-sets to being more independent and interdependent. This process of teachers thinking together and striving to reach shared goals resulted in the staff gaining access to working in more highly collaborative ways. When working through these issues, the staff noted that some of their "problem-solving processes" were ineffective because faculty and staff had a great deal of pride in being perfect. This pride made it difficult at times to admit particular weaknesses. However, once their "foolish pride" was named and exposed, there began a process of becoming liberated from this obstacle. Teachers began joking about their own hidden areas of weakness that they had previously covered up. Teachers even began to say to students, "I don't know the answer to your question. Let's find out together." Eventually it became common to hear teachers apologize to students when they had made a mistake.

The school now continues to systematically and intentionally build its culture. This has required an initial investment of energy, but the investment is paying off. Students are showing more ownership in their learning. Old and tired traditions have been eliminated, and new ones have been established. Previously vexing issues are being addressed at the root level, resulting in increased staff confidence and energy. The school looks cleaner and brighter, and there is an abundance of positive energy that has ignited student voice. And the state test scores, which had been flat for two years, have begun to rise!

RESOURCE A: SCHOOL CULTURE SURVEY

Laneer Middle School Culture Survey   Exit this survey >>

1. Laneer Middle School Culture Survey

This 10-minute survey is designed to identify strengths of your school culture as well as areas to be further developed. All responses are anonymous, and results will be shared with school staff. Thank you for taking the time to provide this valuable feedback.
NOTE: Open a new browser window for each person taking the survey on the same computer.

1. Our school is heading in the right direction.

Strongly Disagree 1	2	3	4	Strongly Agree 5

2. I like working in this school.

Strongly Disagree 1	2	3	4	Strongly Agree 5

3. We are effectively moving students toward meeting district academic goals. (Scores are improving on CSAPS and on other assessments.)

Strongly Disagree 1	2	3	4	Strongly Agree 5

(Continued)

(Continued)

4. The principal fosters constructive dialogue. (He/she brings issues to the faculty and invites their input.)

Strongly Disagree 1	2	3	4	Strongly Agree 5

5. Our school fosters student engagement in academic learning. (For instance, teachers differentiate instruction, encourage student participation, offer choices in assigments when possible, and promote hands-on learning.)

Strongly Disagree 1	2	3	4	Strongly Agree 5

6. I feel safe speaking to the principal—either privately or publicly—about school issues, including those that might be awkward and/or unpopular.

Strongly Disagree 1	2	3	4	Strongly Agree 5

7. Our school effectively engages parents/guardians. (For instance, we regularly send communications home—including positive phone calls, invite parents/guardians to school events, and provide specific guidance for how to support their children academically.)

Strongly Disagree 1	2	3	4	Strongly Agree 5

8. Our staff has a voice in decision making.

Strongly   Strongly
Disagree 1   2   3   4   Agree 5

9. As a staff, we follow through on things we commit to. (For instance, we follow through on our discipline policy and teach our curriculum with fidelity.)

Strongly   Strongly
Disagree 1   2   3   4   Agree 5

10. As a school, we actively promote our shared values. (For instance, we regularly reference the school touchstone or creed.)

Strongly   Strongly
Disagree 1   2   3   4   Agree 5

11. As a staff, we effectively collaborate with one another. (For instance, we regularly review student work together, share ideas and teaching resources, and volunteer to serve on school committees.)

Strongly   Strongly
Disagree 1   2   3   4   Agree 5

(Continued)

(Continued)

12. The staff in this school trust one another.

Strongly Disagree 1	2	3	4	Strongly Agree 5
◡	◡	◡	◡	◡

13. There is a culture of respect at this school among students, staff, parents, and the administration.

Strongly Disagree 1	2	3	4	Strongly Agree 5
◡	◡	◡	◡	◡

14. What do you like best about working at this school?

15. What is the most important issue facing the school?

16. The support I need to help my students learn more is . . . (Try to be realistic!)

Done >>

THE INTENTIONAL SCHOOL CULTURE

The School Touchstone

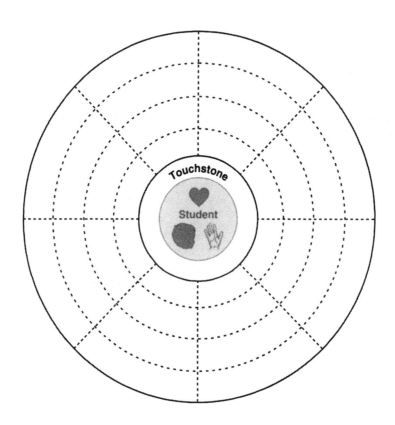

2

The School Touchstone

The schoolwide touchstone is a central tool for shaping an intentional school culture. The touchstone is crafted by the school community and contains universal principles to guide daily decision making, behavior, and reflection. It may serve as a reminder to maintain a sense of humor, as it does at Cory Elementary, or to inspire students and staff to "take the high road," as it does at Slavens School, or to "engage in courageous conversations," as it does at Westerly Creek.

Students thrive when they are immersed in an environment defined by shared universal values. Many students attend schools where the values and expectations differ from classroom to classroom and hallway to hallway. This can be confusing to students and demoralizing to staff, who feel undermined by their colleagues. Without consensus on values, students learn to respond to the values and expectations of each individual teacher but do not develop an affinity for shared school values, since there appear to be none. This helps explain why students can behave so poorly outside their own classroom, such as in the hallways or on the playground or when a substitute teacher is in charge.

"I've come to a frightening conclusion that I am the decisive element in the classroom. It's my personal approach that creates the climate. It's my daily mood that makes the weather. As a teacher, I possess a tremendous power to make a child's life miserable or joyous. I can be a tool of torture or an instrument of inspiration. I can humiliate or humor, hurt or heal. In all situations, it is my response that decides whether a crisis will be escalated or de-escalated and a child humanized or de-humanized.
—*Haim Ginott, teacher, child psychologist, and author*

Educator William Damon noted in his June 19, 2002, White House "talk" about character and community that "children take values seriously only when they perceive at least a rough consensus on them among the adults whom they respect." A touchstone can make this a reality. If together the adults fail to lead in shaping positive values in the school culture, then other qualities, such as injustice, intimidation, and fear, may take root.

A touchstone is not a set of commandments or a mission statement or vision statement. Commandments tend to motivate people out of guilt and fear and may actually reduce intrinsic motivation. A *mission* statement states the purpose of an organization (e.g., "To provide a high-quality education to all students in Johnson Middle School"); a *vision* statement states its goals ("To be number one in the district in math and literacy achievement by 2008").

A touchstone expresses the "how" of an organization, including how to treat each other and the attitudes needed to approach learning and work. It is meant to inspire individuals to be their best and to guide their thoughts and actions on a daily basis. The goal is for students to become intrinsically motivated to live the values of the touchstone. It is not a tool for adults to gain compliance from students.

In more general terms, a touchstone is a test for a standard, such as for the purity of gold. Here, it is a test for how well your thoughts and actions align with the school's core values. And it applies to all members of the school community, not just the students. For instance, at a charter school in Denver staff members rate themselves twice a year on how well they are upholding the values of the school. Parents might be asked the same thing. (See Resource C.)

"School districts should not try to simply build a learning community that has as many definitions as there are people defining it. The emphasis should be on restructuring how people work together. That's what ultimately has an effect on the classroom."
—Nelda Cambron-McCabe, author, in LaFee (2005), p. 6

Businesses have been using touchstones for years. For example, Toyota has developed a highly effective culture, partly by following the Toyota Way, a standard that expresses "how" employees should approach their work.

We accept challenges with a creative spirit and the courage to realize our own dreams without losing drive or energy. We approach our work vigorously, with optimism and a sincere belief in the value of our contribution. We strive to decide our own fate. We act with self-reliance, trusting in our own abilities. We accept responsibility for our conduct and for maintaining and improving the skills that enable us to produce added value. (Liker, 2004, p. 25)

This touchstone is introduced at training sessions for new employees and is posted throughout the workplace and helps define the Toyota philosophy. Specific work practices flow from this corporate philosophy.

For instance, Toyota is committed to getting to the root of problems and not just fixing symptoms. Therefore, employees are trained to ask five times why a problem exists, aiming to get closer to the root problem with each question. Compare this with many other companies that don't have such a process in place and therefore tend to deal with problems only on a surface level. Also, compare it with many schools that fail to get to the root problems of student learning and behavior issues when students are young.

Toyota also teaches its employees to be exceedingly thoughtful in planning new projects, such as the hybrid Prius, but to execute rapidly and to completely support the team. Again, compare this with many other organizations that fail to thoughtfully plan and then waste time in haphazard implementation.

One of the major themes of the Toyota philosophy, which flows into many of its practices, is the belief that the company is always growing, learning, and emerging. They are always looking for new and better ways to reach their goals. Stagnation is not an option. Imagine how much healthier our schools would be if we adopted the same philosophy. If we did, we might also be more willing to get to the root of issues and search for creative solutions.

"Restructuring or setting new standards will not achieve the level of success that reformers hope for without . . . reculturing schools and classrooms."
—Terrence Deal and Kent Peterson, authors (1999), p. 30

For example, when a first grader begins to exhibit persistent behavioral problems, we need to get to the root cause of this behavior and to teach tools of self-control. Too often we address their behavior only at a surface level, resulting in years of disciplining a particular child. This is not good for the school or for the student. Author Hill Walker (Walker, Ramsey, & Gresham, 2003) refers to a study that found that first-grade aggressive boys who were assigned to a "chaotic" classroom were 59 times more likely to be highly aggressive by middle school than their less aggressive peers, compared with aggressive first graders assigned to an orderly classroom, who were only three times more likely than their peers to be aggressive by middle school. This study highlights the importance of thoughtful early intervention.

Top universities also develop and use a touchstone. When James W. Wagner took over the helm of Emory University in 2003, he sought input from the entire university community to craft a statement reflecting the values and direction of the university. Input from hundreds of individuals identified statements and values that reflected what was important to the university. Some of those statements are the following:

- Fostering lifelong learning among all constituents
- Being inquiry driven
- Nurturing creativity
- Engaging in productive partnerships

- Being distinctive for its ethical commitment
- Fostering openness and diversity of thought, experience, and culture
- Working for positive transformation
- Nurturing and celebrating an unusual degree of collegiality and community

The final draft, which incorporates many of the above values and statements, is as follows:

Emory: A destination university internationally recognized as an inquiry-driven, ethically engaged, and diverse community, whose members work collaboratively for positive transformation in the world through courageous leadership in teaching, research, scholarship, health care, and social action.

Emory has done several things to bring power to its touchstone. Values and sometimes actual phrases from the touchstone are embedded in the university's strategic plan, which also was created with the input of thousands in the university community. Also, by deliberately using phrases such as "inquiry-driven, "ethically engaged," and "positive transformation" in speeches and publications, President Wagner and other university leaders have made the touchstone part of the vocabulary of the university.

If the touchstone is properly introduced and developed, students will start holding themselves and their peers accountable for living its values. You might hear an eighth grader at Place Middle School tell a new student "talking trash" in the hallway, "Hey, that's not the Place Way." Without something like the Place Way, students might not feel justified in nudging their peers, partly because they may not feel clear enough about their own values.

We surveyed students at several schools that had integrated their touchstone into their culture. We asked the students if they thought that other schools should develop a touchstone and if they could think of a time when the touchstone impacted their behavior. Almost unanimously, the students recommended that other schools develop a touchstone, and many students could point to specific moments when the touchstone proved valuable. One student described how he was angry at a friend on the playground but chose words over violence because he thought of the touchstone; another student recalled a conversation with his mother just the night before about "taking responsibility for your learning," a phrase drawn from the touchstone magnet on the refrigerator and how this encouraged him to finish his homework. Perhaps the most moving responses, however, came from students who report seeing themselves with new eyes as a result of the touchstone. One student said: "I used to be a bad kid. But since the Lowry Way, I feel like a new person inside." This statement surprised even us, but it shows what can happen when we adults come together and immerse students in an environment that unashamedly promotes positive values. Here's an example:

> ### The Place Way
>
> At Place Middle School, we pursue excellence in scholarship and character. We celebrate and honor each other by being respectful, honest, kind, and fair. We show our cultural appreciation for each other in all we do. We give our best in and out of the classroom and take responsibility for our actions. This is who we are even when no one is watching.

The touchstone can be incorporated into a school by displaying it in all classrooms, by printing it on student ID cards, by sending a printed refrigerator magnet home to parents, and by conducting a school community signing ceremony. It should be an ever-present part of the school. For example, Ellis Elementary School introduces character education stories into school announcements, and the ED (emotionally disturbed) classroom presented a segment of the Ellis Creed to the entire school at a recent assembly. At Dora Moore, a K–8 school, the entire student population gathers once a month to incorporate cross-age learning about each character trait and to develop a strong sense of community. Stedman School holds monthly assemblies with skits written by the kids that explore community issues related to the school creed. The school also is exploring how restorative discipline and service learning complement the values of its touchstone.

A teacher at Lowry Elementary School reflected on how her school introduced its touchstone to its students, which included having students participate in a play about the values in the touchstone. She wrote the following:

Everyone loved it. Then banners and posters were ordered along with the magnets. They arrived a few weeks later and we were ready to somehow present it to students. This is when we ran into trouble. We knew we wanted the introduction of the touchstone to be special and have meaning as well as be fun and memorable. The challenge was what to do? It was decided that we would hire a small acting company for $150 to perform "The Lowry Way." They incorporated our touchstone into their production of "Jack and the Beanstalk" and used Lowry students to act out most of the parts. It was a fabulous way to get the students of all ages involved in the presentation. At the end, Jack and the giant learned the touchstone and agreed to live by "The Lowry Way." Then the student council representatives from each classroom signed "The Lowry Way" banner. Afterwards each classroom teacher invited their students to the sign the banner. "Lowry Way" posters were distributed throughout the school. Each teacher was asked to review "the way" and remind students that this is how we need to conduct ourselves at school as well as at home and in the community. In addition, "The Lowry Way" is recited daily throughout the school.

We include a "distillation" process to help each school develop its own touchstone. Since buy-in and ownership is crucial, it's important to include teachers, parents, and students when developing shared values. One teacher notes: "Little did we know how differently our staff, parents, and students would articulate their ideas. When we entered the touchstone distillation process we understood the meaning of the power of three, but we soon discovered what happens when staff, parents, and students join forces." (See Resource B.)

The distillation process can take time, but it is necessary. It is unwise to hammer out a touchstone in one short meeting. On the other hand, consensus on the actual wording of a touchstone should be defined as what everyone can live with. Otherwise a staff can haggle fruitlessly for months over wording. Make sure that the values selected are a balance of academic and ethical qualities. For instance, phrases such as "We take responsibility for our learning" or "We thirst for learning and academic achievement" communicate the importance of academic learning.

Some schools decide to create a motto that serves as shorthand for the touchstone. For instance, students at Slavens School know that "take the high road" really means to live the whole set of touchstone values. Keep this in mind when crafting a school touchstone—is there a line or phrase that might serve as a motto?

We also recommend that schools create rubrics based on each touchstone value. For example, what does it mean for students and adults at Place Middle School to show "cultural appreciation for each other in all we do"? What are observable behaviors that reflect a high degree of cultural appreciation? A low degree?

We worked with one school where "awareness" was a key value. However, when we began to build rubrics, it became clear there was no consensus among teachers about what they really meant by this concept. One teacher thought it related to emotional self-awareness, and another thought it meant being aware of traffic before you crossed the street. It's hard to nurture "aware" kids when the teachers have such different targets!

Building rubrics and identifying strategies for growth can help clarify for students and adults what the targets are and how to reach them. One elementary school includes photos of students engaged in the desired behaviors. For example, one photo depicts a student turning in homework, which corresponds to a behavior under the rubric for "responsibility." These pictures are especially helpful in communicating touchstone values and behaviors to younger students. We present several sample rubrics in the Resources section at the end of this chapter. (See Resources G and H.)

In addition, we include a Touchstone Effectiveness Assessment tool (see Resource I) to help a school determine how effectively the touchstone is integrated into its culture. A school might realize that it has done little more than hang posters of the touchstone on walls in classrooms and therefore are receiving little value from it. On the other hand, a school might celebrate the many ways it brings life to the touchstone on a daily or weekly basis. We have divided practices into those that increase the visibility of the touchstone, those that enhance its integration into academics, and those that impact behavior and discipline practice. Schools are encouraged to take the instrument at regular intervals to chart progress.

We include a three-part diagram (see Resource C) that shows how a touchstone serves to guide thinking and acting. The touchstone serves as the reference point for helping a student (1) perceive and understand a situation, (2) act skillfully, and (3) reflect and learn from that situation. A skilled teacher, for example, might use this model to help a student identify what "taking the high road" looks like in a particular situation—say, on the playground—and then help him reflect on his actions. Or a parent at Hill Middle School could help her son identify what "taking responsibility for our own learning and behavior" might look like in light of an upcoming field trip. No two situations are exactly alike, and the touchstone can help guide thinking and acting in each one.

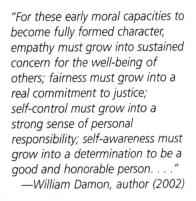

"For these early moral capacities to become fully formed character, empathy must grow into sustained concern for the well-being of others; fairness must grow into a real commitment to justice; self-control must grow into a strong sense of personal responsibility; self-awareness must grow into a determination to be a good and honorable person. . . ."
—William Damon, author (2002)

The touchstone becomes the "north star" of a school and helps guide the daily decision making of students and staff. It can also inform decisions about many aspects of school life, including parental involvement, afterschool programs, and the hiring of staff. A creed such as the Toyota Way or Emory University statement of values is the glue that holds successful organizations together and keeps them focused, even during turbulent times.

RESOURCE B: SAMPLE PROCEDURE FOR DISTILLING SCHOOLWIDE INPUT IN SHAPING A SCHOOL TOUCHSTONE

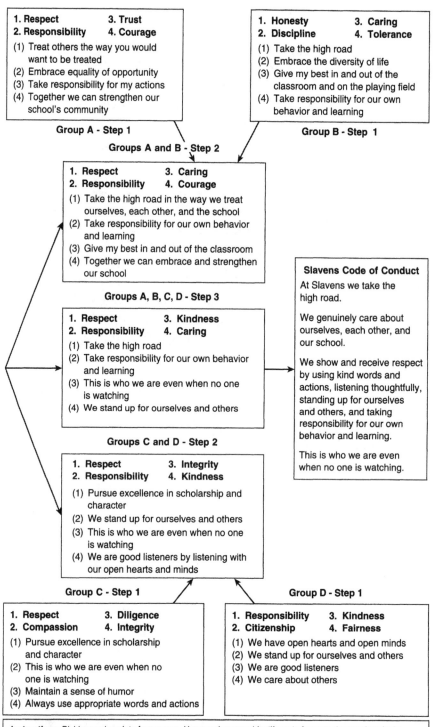

Group A - Step 1

1. Respect   3. Trust
2. Responsibility   4. Courage

(1) Treat others the way you would want to be treated
(2) Embrace equality of opportunity
(3) Take responsibility for my actions
(4) Together we can strengthen our school's community

Group B - Step 1

1. Honesty   3. Caring
2. Discipline   4. Tolerance

(1) Take the high road
(2) Embrace the diversity of life
(3) Give my best in and out of the classroom and on the playing field
(4) Take responsibility for our own behavior and learning

Groups A and B - Step 2

1. Respect   3. Caring
2. Responsibility   4. Courage

(1) Take the high road in the way we treat ourselves, each other, and the school
(2) Take responsibility for our own behavior and learning
(3) Give my best in and out of the classroom
(4) Together we can embrace and strengthen our school

Groups A, B, C, D - Step 3

1. Respect   3. Kindness
2. Responsibility   4. Caring

(1) Take the high road
(2) Take responsibility for our own behavior and learning
(3) This is who we are even when no one is watching
(4) We stand up for ourselves and others

Slavens Code of Conduct

At Slavens we take the high road.

We genuinely care about ourselves, each other, and our school.

We show and receive respect by using kind words and actions, listening thoughtfully, standing up for ourselves and others, and taking responsibility for our own behavior and learning.

This is who we are even when no one is watching.

Groups C and D - Step 2

1. Respect   3. Integrity
2. Responsibility   4. Kindness

(1) Pursue excellence in scholarship and character
(2) We stand up for ourselves and others
(3) This is who we are even when no one is watching
(4) We are good listeners by listening with our open hearts and minds

Group C - Step 1

1. Respect   3. Diligence
2. Compassion   4. Integrity

(1) Pursue excellence in scholarship and character
(2) This is who we are even when no one is watching
(3) Maintain a sense of humor
(4) Always use appropriate words and actions

Group D - Step 1

1. Responsibility   3. Kindness
2. Citizenship   4. Fairness

(1) We have open hearts and open minds
(2) We stand up for ourselves and others
(3) We are good listeners
(4) We care about others

Instructions: Divide members into four groups. Have each person identify up to four prominent values in the school and up to four phrases or sentences that might fit into the creed. Have each group agree on four shared values and four phrases or sentences. Pair up Groups A and B as well as C and D and do the same. Keep synthesizing until you agree on a master set of values and phrases. Construct the creed based on this master list.

**RESOURCE C: HOW A SCHOOL TOUCHSTONE CAN GUIDE THINKING
                AND ACTING**

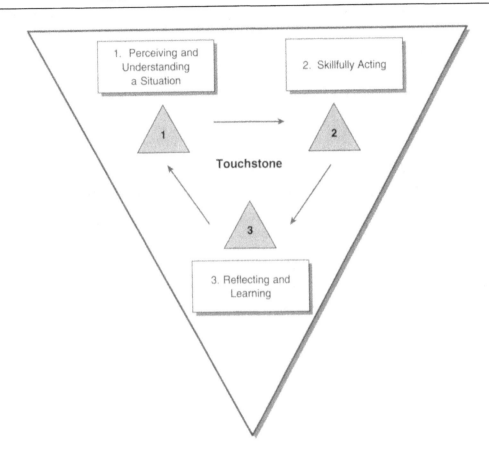

As this diagram indicates, an individual is constantly in relationship with the touchstone and a concrete situation. Ideally, the touchstone serves as a reference point for all three phases of ethical action:

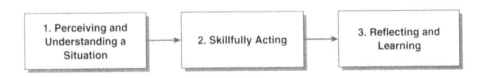

(Continued)

RESOURCE C   (Continued)

For example, let's look at how the touchstone might guide the thinking and acting of a student at Hill Middle School. Recall, Hill's touchstone is the following:

The Skyhawk Creed

At Hill, we are connected by common goals:

- Achieving academic excellence through hard work
- Respecting each other by using kind words and actions
- Taking responsibility for our own learning and behavior

We know that it takes courage to live this creed, especially when no one is watching!

Situation: Imagine that Mary, a 7th grader, hears rumors during lunchtime about Dana, a new girl at school, and Mary knows that these rumors might damage Dana's reputation. Below is a diagram of how the Skyhawk Creed might serve as a useful guide for Mary in this situation.

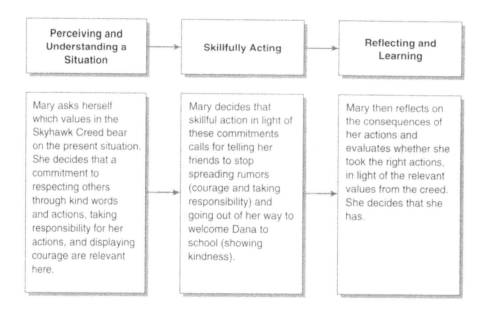

RESOURCE D: CASE EXAMPLES

A living creed or touchstone can be a powerful tool for building community in an organization; members tend to feel more connected to each other when joined by common values.

Slavens School

At Slavens, a K–8 school in Denver, a committee of parents, teachers, and the principal met for nearly a year to read various books and articles about character and character education. After soliciting input from teachers, students, and parents, they crafted the following code of conduct:

> ### Slavens Code of Conduct
>
> *At Slavens we take the high road.*
> *We genuinely care about ourselves, each other, and our school.*
> *We show and receive respect by: using kind words and actions, listening*
>   *thoughtfully, standing up for ourselves and others, and taking*
>   *responsibility for our own behavior and learning.*
> *This is who we are even when no one is watching!*

Cory Elementary

Initially, Cory formed a character-education committee consisting of parents, teachers, and the principal. After gaining background knowledge on character education and sending a climate survey out to the community, the committee began working on a touchstone. They put a large piece of butcher paper outside each classroom with two headings: "Things we should preserve and celebrate at Cory," and "Things we can improve at Cory." The committee solicited similar feedback at parent and community meetings. Based on this input, the committee created the Cory Creed.

> ### The Cory Creed
>
> *At Cory we love learning and laughter.*
> *We grow by trying new things and learning from our mistakes.*
> *We embrace challenges with the courage to do our best.*
> *We persevere.*
> *We show respect for our community through caring, responsible actions.*
> *We celebrate each other's differences and accomplishments.*
> *At Cory we love learning and laughter.*

RESOURCE E: TOUCHSTONE SIGNING CEREMONY

A touchstone contains agreed-upon principles that guide daily decision making and behavior, bringing coherence to how things are done in the school.

After the touchstone has been developed by the school community and materials (magnets, posters, and the banner) have been ordered and received, it is time for implementation. The School Culture Committee creates a plan for the Touchstone Signing Ceremony and ongoing integration. It is ideal if the ceremony occurs at the beginning of the school year. Several questions the committee should consider are: How can we integrate the touchstone into our school culture? How can we create a touchstone kick-off event that will be inspiring, personally meaningful, and unifying for students and staff?

The Touchstone Presentation Ceremony
(as an assembly or in subgroups)

- Decide if the entire school community (all grades) will meet at the same time, by grade-level groupings (lower and upper elementary) or grade by grade.
- Determine the mood of the ceremony. Do you want it to be a festive celebration or a dignified, earnest event?
- Consider including music, arts, drama, color guard, and multimedia.
- Invite parents and community members to sit in the back and witness (but not sign).
- Include early childhood education and kindergarten students in the ceremony, but let them know they will have the opportunity to sign when they are in first grade (something to look forward to).
- Consider inviting a guest speaker (a notable community member, an Office of Character and School Culture staff person, etc.) to speak briefly and/or shake students' hands.
- Invite local media to cover the event. Submit photos and a story to local papers.
- Share that the touchstone is not just for students, it is for *all* staff.
- Present or discuss the meaning of the touchstone, piece by piece. Provide an opportunity for students to ask questions. Give examples of what "living" the touchstone looks like in the classroom, halls, cafeteria, and other school areas.
- Explain that each student will have a choice to sign or not. There is no pressure. Before signing, each person needs to (1) understand what the touchstone means, and (2) be willing to live by the touchstone principles.
- Distribute magnets to parents and guardians at a back-to-school night or other school function, or allow students to take the magnets home the day of the signing ceremony.

The Signing Ceremony

- Arrange (preferably on the same day) for students to go to the library or to an open room in which students will choose to sign or witness others signing. *If the Touchstone Presentation Ceremony is done grade by grade (in small groups), the actual signing may happen at that time.*
- Consider starting with a poem or a story, such as *Teammates* by Peter Golenbock and Paul Bacon. Hold a brief discussion about how this relates to the touchstone.
- Communicate that signing is optional. There is no pressure to do so, and each person should be fully aware of what and why they are signing. Students need to know that if they choose not to sign that day, they will have an opportunity later.
- Provide clear directions regarding the size of their signatures. (You may create a stencil border to keep signatures to a uniform size to ensure there is enough room on the banner for all, plus any new students who will enter the school.) Conduct an annual recommitment ceremony at the start of each school year. Students may sign a poster board that is displayed near the banner, indicating their recommitment.

Visibility

- Display the signed banner in a prominent location.
- Ensure that touchstone posters are displayed in all classrooms as well as in the cafeteria, gym, offices, halls, meetings rooms, and so forth. Some schools choose to create murals or artistically represent the touchstone throughout the building.
- Create a ritual where the entire school community recites the touchstone as a part of morning announcements—ideally led by students over the PA on a daily or weekly basis.
- Include the touchstone in the school's parent and student newspapers. Offer tips on how parents may integrate the touchstone at home.
- Start all school functions with participants reciting the touchstone.
- Include the touchstone in student planners on the backs of identification cards.

Ongoing Development

- Develop a plan for introducing and providing an opportunity for new students to sign the touchstone. This might be led by older students and occur once a month.
- Ensure that the parents of a new student receive a touchstone magnet when registering.

(Continued)

RESOURCE E   (Continued)

- Bring teachers together as an entire school or by grade level to discuss how the touchstone will be integrated into the academic curriculum.
- Develop a shared agreement for how the touchstone will be referenced in behavioral incidents (refocus forms, restorative discipline, student and parental meetings).
- Create an awards program to recognize students and staff who exemplify living the principles of the touchstone. Provide public recognition.

Measuring the Effectiveness of Touchstone

- Use the Touchstone Effectiveness Assessment (included).
- Create rubrics indicating the specific behaviors that are expected (based on the touchstone), and use it to reflect on and then create strategies for improvement, individually or collectively as a class.

RESOURCE F: POSTER FOR TOUCHSTONE KICK-OFF

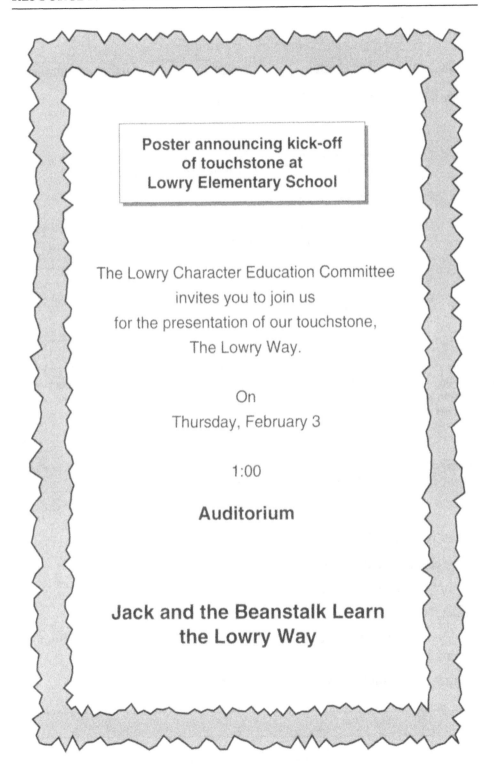

Poster announcing kick-off
of touchstone at
Lowry Elementary School

The Lowry Character Education Committee
invites you to join us
for the presentation of our touchstone,
The Lowry Way.

On
Thursday, February 3

1:00

Auditorium

Jack and the Beanstalk Learn
the Lowry Way

RESOURCE G: SAMPLE OF STUDENT TOUCHSTONE RUBRIC (1)

Problem Solvers

Undeveloped	Developing	Proficient	Highly Accomplished
Chooses not to listen	Sometimes listens	Usually listens	Always listens
Reacts without thinking	Sometimes thinks before reacting	Usually thinks before reacting	Always thinks before reacting
Uses violence to solve problems	Doesn't try to solve own problems	Usually solves problems peacefully	Always solves problems peacefully
Doesn't ask questions	Sometimes asks thoughtful questions	Usually asks thoughtful questions	Asks thoughtful questions
Has difficulty understanding what a problem is and therefore cannot solve	Sometimes sees others' points of view in decision making	Usually sees others' points of view in decision making	Able to look at many sides without judgment to make decisions
Usually instigates problems	Sometimes instigates problems	Rarely instigates problems	Never instigates problems

Strategies for Growth

1. Model active listening skills.
2. Count to ten before reacting.
3. Take five deep breaths.
4. Student court—Older students will listen to disputes and voice their opinions.
5. Think about the five W's—Who? What? When? Where? Why?
6. _____
7. _____
8. _____
9. _____

RESOURCE H: SAMPLE OF STUDENT TOUCHSTONE RUBRIC (2)

"We respect ourselves, each other, our school, and our community."

	Undeveloped	*Developing*	*Highly Accomplished*
Definitions	You are disrespectful. You don't take care of the school, yourself, or your friends.	You appreciate your own value and the value of others and their property. You are aware of others' needs. You care about your friends. You know what's right and have learned to believe in yourself.	You have great self-confidence. You believe in yourself and in others. You take pride in yourself, your school, and your community and look for ways to make them better.
When it comes to littering . . .			
Example	You don't pick up after yourself in class, at lunch, at recess, or at home.	You take care of your own trash and clean up after yourself.	You pick up any trash you see and come up with a plan to reduce trash (e.g., recycling).
When it comes to teasing and bullying . . .			
Example	You tease and bully other kids.	You don't tease, bully, or pick on others because you know it's wrong.	You never bully or tease and don't allow anyone else to either. If you see someone being bullied or teased, stick up for that person.
When it comes to how you treat yourself . . .			
Example	You think you're not good enough to play or participate. You call yourself names. You'll say, "I'm so stupid. I can't do anything!"	You are gentle with yourself. You take care of your body by exercising, eating healthy foods, and getting enough sleep.	You believe in yourself. You can do it! You care about your body and your mind. You find ways to take care of your body, mind, and spirit.

RESOURCE I: TOUCHSTONE EFFECTIVENESS ASSESSMENT

	Rarely/never or "no" (0)	Sometimes (1)	Usually/always or "yes" (2)
Visibility			
The touchstone is read over the intercom at least once a week. Consider having students do this.			
The school has created magnets of the touchstone and sent them home to parents.			
The touchstone is printed on important school documents, such as newsletters, student planners, ID cards, and so forth.			
The touchstone is integrated into assemblies and other schoolwide events.			
The touchstone is displayed in all classrooms.			
The school had a signing ceremony and now has an annual recommitment ceremony.			
Academics			
Teachers integrate the touchstone into literacy, social studies, and other relevant subject areas.			
Teachers weave themes of the touchstone into writing assignments.			
Behavior and Discipline			
Teachers and administrators reference the touchstone during conferences with students and during discipline discussions.			
The touchstone is printed on forms relating to discipline, such as refocus forms and forms relating to restorative discipline.			

	Rarely/never or "no" (0)	Sometimes (1)	Usually/always or "yes" (2)
Other			
Teachers meet either in small teams or as a faculty to discuss ways to further integrate the touchstone into the school.			
The school has a plan to introduce the touchstone to students who enroll later in the school year.			
The majority of the students can recite the touchstone.			
Date: **Total number of points:**			
Strong implementation. Congratulations! Keep up the good work, and seek out ways to keep the touchstone fresh.	18–26 points		
Medium implementation. You're off to a good start, but there is more you can do to gain power from your touchstone.	12–17 points		
Beginning implementation. It's unlikely that your touchstone is helping your culture. Consider adding one or two practices immediately to bolster its power.	11 or fewer points		

RESOURCE J: TOUCHSTONE MAGNETS

At Fallis Elementary, we stand by each other to create a caring community of lifelong learners.

- We honor and respect individual differences.
- We take responsibility for our learning and our actions.
- We communicate with each other in a caring, honest, and positive way.
- We learn with a smile and a joyful attitude.

If you can imagine it, you can achieve it!

Dora Moore K–8 School

We are a community working together to promote educational success.

We are respectful, supportive, responsible, honest, hardworking, courteous, and kind.

Our efforts create an environment that is safe, inviting, and productive.

We have confidence in ourselves and our achievements.

Expect More   Learn More   Be More

Barrett Touchstone

At Barrett, I am in charge of my learning.
At Barrett, I am responsible for my actions and my words.
At Barrett, I respect and treat people nicely.
At Barrett, I choose to do the right thing.

This is who I am even when no one is watching.

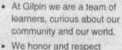

The Lowry Way

At Lowry, we create opportunities to soar.
At Lowry, we take responsibility for our education.
At Lowry, we embrace our lives with compassion for each other.
At Lowry, we strive to do our best and help others along the way.
At Lowry, we show respect by fostering honesty and integrity.
At Lowry, we love learning and we have fun!!!!

At Edison we are . . .

Community-minded
Aware
Responsible
Respectful
Empathetic
Safe

Together we learn. Together we grow.
Together we achieve.

The Edison Community CARES!

The Gilpin Way

- At Gilpin we are a team of learners, curious about our community and our world.
- We honor and respect ourselves and others around us.
- We pledge to take responsibility for our actions, for our learning, and for creating a caring and positive environment.
- We build a better future and a lifetime of accomplishments.

Gilpin Jaguars roar with pride!

The Griffin Touchstone

Griffins have the courage to persevere when
  faced with a challenge and the integrity to
  choose the right path.

We are scholars.
We take responsibility for our education.
We value diversity because we have respect
  for ourselves and others.

This is how we show loyalty to each other,
  our school, and our community.

The Cory Creed

At Cory we love learning and laughter.
We grow by trying new things and learning from
  our mistakes.
We embrace challenges with the courage to
  do our best.
We persevere.
We show respect for our community through
  caring, responsible actions.
We celebrate each other's differences and
  accomplishments.

At Cory, we love learning and laughter.

Oh, The Things We Can Learn at Centennial . . .

Imagine a school of
successful and responsible citizens . . .

  Learning with eagerness and pride . . .
  Living with kindness and respect.

Let's imagine it, learn it, and live it together!

Ah, Las Cosas Que Podemos Aprender en Centennial . . .

Imaginate una escuela de
ciudadanos exitosos y responsables . . .

  Que estudian satisfechos y con ansias
  de aprender . . .
  Que viven con amabilidad y respeto.

¡Vamos a imaginárnosla, a aprender así y a
vivirla juntos!

The Teller Promise

At Teller, we learn and laugh together.

We respect each other by using kind
words and actions.

We take responsibility for our own learning
and behavior, even when no one is watching.

At Teller, we celebrate each other's differences
and accomplishments.

The Wyman Way

Wyman Wildcats are a family and we strive
  for excellence.

We set high goals and work hard to reach them.

We are learners and we help each other learn.

We accept new challenges and learn from
  our mistakes.

We are kind and we take care of each other.

Wyman Wildcats are a family.

SOURCES: Fallis Elementary School, Dora Moore School, Barrett Elementary School, Lowry Elementary School, Edison Elementary School, Gilpin Elementary School, The Griffin Touchstone, Cory Elementary School, Centennial Elementary School, Teller Elementary School, and Wyman Elementary School.

THE INTENTIONAL SCHOOL CULTURE

The Four Mind-Set Model

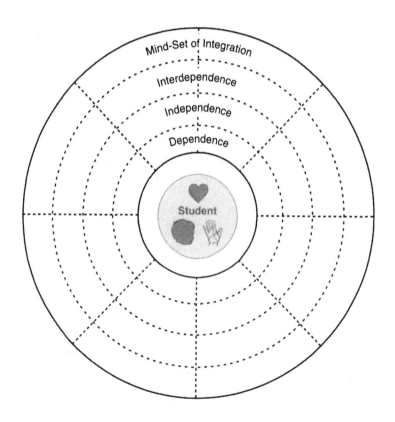

3

The Four Mind-Set Model

W e have made the case for deliberately shaping a school culture and have introduced the touchstone as a valuable tool in that process. We now turn to the Four Mind-Set Model, which describes how the work of schooling can be approached from four different mind-sets: dependence, independence, interdependence, and integration. Since mind-sets help shape our reality, the mind-set from which each of the key stakeholders operates—students, parents, and staff—can have a profound impact on school culture and on student performance.

Mental models shape how we view the world and can be described as our "lenses" on the world. As Peter Senge (1990) writes in the *The Fifth Discipline*, "Mental models are deeply ingrained assumptions, generalizations, or even pictures and images that influence how we understand and how we take action" (p. 8). When we access more expansive mental models, we can see reality in more expansive ways and then act in ways that lead to better results. (See Resource K.) For instance, some people might operate under a mental model based on competition that encourages them to see interactions in the world exclusively from a zero-sum perspective: that is, someone wins at the expense of another losing. Using only this lens, people always would behave in ways that increased their chances of "winning" and others of losing. On the other hand, were they to expand the mental model to include the concept of collaboration, the range of possible actions would grow. People would not have to abandon their competitive behaviors—which might be appropriate in some settings—but would be able to act out of a larger world view that now includes the well-being of others. We believe there is value in understanding the benefits and limitations of the mental model one is generally working under and being aware of the other model possibilities.

The mind-set of *dependence* holds the qualities of acceptance, humility, and respect: respect for tradition, respect for rules, respect for decorum, and respect for a chain of command. Things get done efficiently and on time, and clear role boundaries are honored when we operate from this orientation. When the school's fire alarm sounds, for instance, this orientation teaches us to swiftly leave the building through a prescribed exit instead of deciding on our own how to respond. This orientation enables teachers to honor the schoolwide disciplinary policy even if it means changing their own approach to discipline. But there are downsides to operating only from this orientation, including a lack of initiative, creativity, and collegiality and an unreflective pursuit of goals.

> "Teachers do have to be dependable and trustworthy, but not to the extent of leading students to deny their own capabilities and become utterly dependent."
> —James Atherton, author (2005)

In our fire alarm example, if we encounter heavy smoke when leading a group of students out of the building, the teacher needs to abandon the designated plans and use his or her best judgment to bring the students to safety. This is the mind-set of *independence*, which embodies initiative and responsibility: responsibility for meeting your goals. For instance, a teacher might design a unique field trip for her students to enhance course content or alter the curriculum to share a passion about a particular period in history. However, the teacher might fail to recognize that this field trip might fit better with the curriculum of the next grade level or she might become so wrapped up in teaching the Civil War that she fails to adequately prepare her students for the following history course. When one operates only from the independent mind-set, the person usually has *the* answer and has personal interpretations of rules, decorum, and respect.

The mind-set of *interdependence* is highlighted when a group of teachers and students find themselves trapped in a smoke-filled building and draw on their collective intelligence and knowledge of the facility and of fire to find safety. This mind-set embraces the energy of caring. At its best, interdependence can help schools address issues by leveraging collective knowledge and wisdom and lead to a heightened sense of connectedness and well-being among the group. Though there are far fewer potential downsides to interdependence than to the other orientations, interdependence could invite too much input for some decisions or the lack of individual initiative, accountability, and even groupthink.

> "The real difficulty in changing the course of any enterprise lies not in developing new ideas but in escaping from the old ones."
> — John Maynard Keynes, British economist and author

The call for a paradigm shift from independent to interdependent thinking and acting is coming from many arenas. Just look for examples like these in today's newspapers:

Patient dies because medical specialists were unaware of one another's treatments. The medical community is searching for a team approach among specialists where the patient is the beneficiary of their best shared insight in healing the whole body through determining the order and the coordination of treating multiple ailments.

In the wake of 9/11, the intelligence services are struggling with overcoming their independent ways of operating as they are trying to implement a collaborative model of sharing so they can build on each other's information.

As a nation, we would do well to make a Declaration of Interdependence!

The fourth mental model, the mind-set of *integration*, involves integrating the best qualities of the three other mind-sets. It is the mind-set of discerning wisdom and skillful means. We tend to work exclusively out of one realm, say, interdependence, and reject the value of other realms. This is unfortunate because sometimes what is called for is a different way of being. Integration prevents us from getting stuck in the rut of acting only one way, which can lead to frustration and ineffective action. Without the awareness that other paradigms are readily available, we believe that reality is bounded by our dominant paradigm, which we vigorously defend. The wisdom inherent from integrating the best qualities of each mind-set as determined by a given situation liberates oneself from the narrow limitations of mind-sets themselves. In the *Re-Enchantment of Learning*, the authors quote Duane Elgin (1993): "We live individually and collectively almost totally embedded within our mentally constructed reality. . . . In the process we lose a large measure of our innate capacity for voluntary, deliberate, intentional action" (quoted in Crowell, Caine, & Caine, 1998, p. 45).

> "We are all caught in an inescapable network of mutuality, tied into a single garment of destiny. Whatever affects one directly, affects all indirectly.
> —Martin Luther King, Jr.

The often-heard statement "seeing is believing" should perhaps be changed to "believing is seeing" since our beliefs shape what we see. We have learned that the mind-set from which we operate matters because our thinking shapes how we make sense of the world and determines our actions. As 19th-century British author William Thackeray wrote:

Sow a thought, reap an act;
Sow an act, reap a habit;
Sow a habit, reap a character;
Sow a character, reap a destiny.

Teachers and the Four Mind-Set Model

In the recent past, teachers and principals have been asked to function independently. Our training, and even the physical layout of our schools, has promoted this way of thinking and acting. Particularly at a secondary level, many teachers have become accustomed to closing their doors and pursuing their own agendas. (See Resource M.)

Teachers are currently struggling with the strong mandates coming from central administration as well as from the state and federal governments. This makes many teachers (and even principals) feel they are losing their independence and are being reduced to a state of dependency. With independence so highly prized by the teaching profession and by American culture in general, many educators see little value in anything resembling dependent behavior—even when it might be appropriate—nor are they aware of the value of interdependence. The two stories below illustrate some of these issues and explore how this model plays out in the lives of teachers.

> "We don't see things as they are, we see things as we are."
> —Anaïs Nin, author

Ms. Olsen has taught fourth grade for eight years. She vividly remembers her first teaching job. She spent two nervous, yet satisfying days at her new school getting her room ready, attending faculty gatherings, and enjoying the warm school climate. On Monday morning, after students arrived for their new school year, not a colleague was in sight. That morning was like the beginning of a race: the bell went off and teachers retreated to their classrooms. Since then she has fended for herself.

Recently, she faced having to implement the Everyday Math curriculum, even though her plate is quite full. (The district already required the use of one literacy program for all its elementary schools.) Ms. Olsen feels that her independence as a professional has deteriorated because of these mandates and hears similar complaints from colleagues. No one conferred with them about new literacy and math curricula. A negative climate continues to grow as each teacher's frustrations are added to the faculty-room conversation. No one is open to the possibility of another way of handling these many challenges and requirements from the district.

The principal seems to be more strident as she feels that she is being reduced to a middle manager, passing edicts from the central office to her faculty. Her sense of autonomy as a leader has been eroded, and, as a result, she is becoming more heavy-handed and authoritarian with staff and students.

The current atmosphere is beginning to affect school culture through less adaptive capacity, less elasticity in dealing with challenges, less creative thinking, and less ownership in the well-being of the school. Some of the frustration can be seen in an increase of teachers yelling at students, less flexibility in working with parents, increased teacher absenteeism, and a loss of faith in the district. At the end of each school day, Ms. Olsen and many of her colleagues leave exhausted. They "crawl out" of school at 4:30 each day only to "crawl back" in at 7:45 the next morning.

Ms. Olsen's school is stuck in an orientation of independence, with little awareness or willingness to think and act in different ways. Let's now look at how another school, faced with similar challenges, responded differently.

When fourth-grade teacher Ms. Duran, her colleagues, and the principal learned that all elementary teachers had to use the Everyday Math curriculum, they didn't waste time fighting the decision. They put their heads together and got to work. They moved quickly to study the new curriculum and dialogued several times about how to implement it most effectively, taking into account the needs of the students, the teachers' capacities for change, relationships with parents, and other relevant considerations. These dialogues were unconstrained and enlisted a wide range of perspectives.

In the third gathering, the staff decided to have one grade-level teacher focus on math instruction and the other teacher focus on literacy. After further research on "platooning" or "teaming," including visiting schools in the area using this strategy, the school successfully integrated the Everyday Math curriculum into the school. This included hosting several parental evenings to introduce the math materials and new learning structures. Teachers established two shared agreements that they felt would keep them on track during this transition and honored these agreements through twice-yearly staff reflections.

Notice how differently the two schools responded to the district mandate to adopt Everyday Math. In one school, the teachers became frayed and exhausted because they tried to respond to the change on their own. Ms. Duran and her colleagues, however, addressed the challenge as a group and from a much more inte-

"Everyone thinks of changing the world, but no one thinks of changing himself."
—Leo Tolstoy, Russian author and philosopher

grated mind-set, resulting in a more effective response. The staff in Ms. Duran's school will likely emerge with more confidence and energy to take on the next educational challenge, whereas those in Ms. Olsen's school will likely emerge with less.

Teachers have not been prepared to work out of this kind of transformative thinking. We struggle with schools in transitioning from rewarding only staff self-sufficiency to rewarding collaboration that fundamentally shifts how things are done at the school. Asking for help should no longer be seen as a weakness but as a sign of commitment to professional growth. We see that schools have gotten as much as they can out of the "do it yourself" paradigm and that working harder out of this paradigm cannot give better results.

Most teacher training prepares teachers for working with children in the classroom but does not prepare teachers for working with colleagues and adults in the schoolhouse or with their students' parents. In addition, teachers have not been prepared to deal with many other parts of the teaching life. They do not know how to heal themselves and colleagues from the losses and wounds of daily school life, they rarely see themselves as *part* of the larger K–12 educational journey taken by students, and they have not been prepared to effectively deal with change itself.

"*Every man takes the limits of his own field of vision for the limits of the world.*"
—*Arthur Schopenhauer, German author and philosopher*

The Four Mind-Set Model can lend insight to the above-mentioned challenges and to the common educational issues and paradoxes listed below. The *dependent* mind-set leaves teachers stuck trying to pursue two seemingly contradictory instructions. *Independent*-minded teachers tend to choose aspects of the paradox that are closest to their liking. *Interdependent*-minded teachers align themselves with the school's agreed-upon balance between the seemingly paradoxical expectations. *Integration*-minded teachers embrace the paradoxical aspects of the school's culture and creatively work with these challenges. Here are some examples:

- Classrooms should be hospitable *and* have an edge or some disequilibrium to promote growth.
- Instruction should be bound by academic standards *and* open to broader exploration and creativity.
- Teachers should be rigorous and demanding in their expectations of student learning *and* provide the pacing to put students on a winning streak.
- Teachers should focus on the teaching of academic standards *and* care for the inner well-being of their students.
- Teachers should feel connected with their students *and* retain a professional relationship.

- Teachers should be leaders in their school *and* follow mandates from administration.
- Teachers should have a strong voice in fostering change *and* be respectful in honoring school traditions and policies.
- Teachers should be knowledgeable professionals *and* should listen to and be in partnership with their students' parents.
- Teachers should know how to help struggling students but teachers do not and cannot always have the answer.
- Teachers should empower their students *and* not feel defensive when their empowered students challenge them.
- Teachers should take an active stake in the success of colleagues *and* have the courage to speak out if a colleague is causing harm to students or the school.

"Oftentimes in teacher education programs we are taught to work with children and not taught how to work with adults. Then more often than not, we go into a class isolated from the rest of the school and become chiefs of our own domain. If we are to work effectively with our colleagues we need to see beyond our classroom and into the school itself."

—Jennifer Abrams, educator

The Four Mind-Set Model can present ways to maximize the best aspects of these seemingly conflicting views by appreciating the wisdom inherent in dependence, independence, and interdependence. For example, a teacher can be dependent on the state academic standards, be open and act independently to a student's request to explore a tangential area, and then work interdependently with the student so the learning has integrity and coherence with the standards.

Students and the Four Mind-Set Model

The Four Mind-Set Model can also be applied to the development of students. (See Resource N.) In his book, *Intellectual Character*, Ron Ritchhart (2002) argues that what stays with students from their education are patterns: "patterns of behavior, patterns of thinking, patterns of interaction" (p. 9). These patterns of thinking can be intentionally shaped. For example, a properly designed school culture can facilitate a developmental shift from dependence to independence to interdependence and ultimately to integrative thinking.

In kindergarten, students learn to raise their hands and wait to be called on, they take turns on the swings, and they stand in line at the drinking fountain. They learn to respect the rules of the school and are largely "dependent" on the adults for their learning. While dependent students may dutifully attend class, turn in assignments, and be able to regurgitate information, they may not have an abiding commitment to learning. They are motivated primarily by extrinsic measures, based on fear of failure and hope for positive rewards.

When these students develop more independence, they take greater responsibility for their own learning, although they still may be focused primarily on "me" and not particularly concerned with the well-being of the larger school community. As their mind-set grows to include interdependency, they begin to contribute to collaborative learning activities and promote the well-being of the school as a whole.

A similar shift might occur in students' relationship with knowledge. At the dependent level, they may simply absorb facts, whereas at the interdependent level they are more able to synthesize information. For example, students might apply a concept from yesterday's math class to a social issue reported on the morning news. Unfortunately some schools keep students stuck in dependency; the healthiest schools expand student mind-sets.

> "We all know that what will transform education is not another theory, another book, or another formula but educators who are willing to seek a transformed way of being in the world."
> —Parker Palmer, author (1999), p. 15

Some faculty members who work primarily out of the independent mind-set tend to keep their students in dependent roles because of issues of power and control. The schools where teachers collaborate and see the interconnectedness of their worlds tend to foster greater student independent and interdependent development. These teachers empower themselves and their students

to see the world in connected ways, to look at ordinary events in the world as a source of joy and relation, to participate creatively and become part of the wonder of life, to learn to function effectively in the midst of process and change, and to see the intricate relationships and expansive possibilities of knowing and being." (Crowell, Caine, & Caine, 1998, p. 152)

In their book *Raising Self-Reliant Children in a Self-Indulgent World: Seven Building Blocks for Developing Capable Young People*, Stephen Glenn and Jane Nelson state that "all children are born at risk to problems of dependency. The perceptions and skills that are necessary for self-reliance and effective living require development and maintenance" (p. 29). The seven building blocks are healthy perceptions of personal capabilities, personal significance, and personal influence over life followed by strong intrapersonal and interpersonal skills, sound judgment, and the capacity to respond effectively to human and natural systems. Glenn and Nelson conclude that "a primary goal of parent and teaching processes is that of strengthening these areas so that our young people can take on life with an adequate base of these personal resources and assets" (p. 30).

Parents and the Four Mind-Set Model

Some parents approach their child's schooling from only a dependent mind-set. (See Resource O.) They might drop their child off at school, trusting the school to take care of their child's educational needs. The parents might not appropriately advocate for their child, such as by asking for extra math challenges or for titles of summer reading books. The parents might not share pertinent information with school, such as the fact their daughter spends three weeks in February with relatives out-of-state.

Parents take more responsibility for their child's education when they operate from a more independent mind-set. In doing so, however, they might act as a special interest group on behalf of their child and demand a particular teacher or rescue their child from having to take responsibility for his or her actions. In this paradigm, parents tend to see themselves exclusively as consumers of the school who are in competition with other families to get the best out of the school.

As parents come to appreciate the value of interdependence, they might contribute time, skills, and/or money to enhance the educational experience of all students. They no longer see the school as a finite resource to compete over but as a potentially expanding resource for the well-being of all young people in the school. Parents begin to ask what they can do for the school instead of the other way around. For instance, instead of raising funds so their daughter's second-grade class can have drama, they raise funds so that all students in the school can benefit from the dramatic arts.

The most effective parents use the best from each mind-set for the benefit of their child and all children, and the best schools help parents do this.

Leadership and the Four Mind-Set Model

School leaders are crucial catalysts for helping members of the school community think and act in more integrated ways. One way a principal can do this is by leading in a more highly integrated manner.

"Progress is impossible without change; and those who cannot change their minds cannot change anything."
—George Bernard Shaw, Irish writer and Nobel Prize winner

If a principal leads only from a mind-set or framework of dependency, she relies too heavily on the power of hierarchy: Teachers and staff do the things the principal asks simply because she is the principal. This might work for a while, but it will eventually lead to resentment and lack of ownership among the staff. It also reinforces other hierarchies in the building—say, between teachers and the support staff—and a tightening of role boundaries (e.g., "That's not my job").

Leading from a mind-set of independence creates a healthier school, but this has problems of its own. From this framework, a principal manages the many different "islands" of the school—the individual teachers, the special programs, the sports teams, and so on—and gives plenty of freedom for each island to flourish. For instance, the school may house an award-winning speech and debate program or a model technology program. On the other hand, the principal might not do enough to help each person see how his or her piece fits into the whole and how he or she can support others' efforts. The principal also may be skilled at generating from staff many possible solutions to pressing issues but less skilled at encouraging follow-through on a common solution. This fragmentation can impact instruction and breed a sense of isolation among teachers.

When a principal leads from a framework of interdependence, she shares power with the whole staff, facilitates collaboration when appropriate, and reinforces that each member is part of the whole. For instance, she may create task forces made of teachers to look into revising certain school policies. Or she may develop a master schedule that enables teachers to meet in teams and provide training to focus these meetings on student work.

The principal also can frame how teachers see their work. For example, teachers can dutifully attend the faculty meeting, passively taking in the information shared by the principal (dependence). Or they can attend with the attitude that it is their personal time to grade papers or gab with a friend during the meeting (independence). Or they can be fully present, understanding the importance of and contributing to the dialogues and decisions and then follow through with coordinated implementation (interdependence). In the first case, the teacher sees faculty meeting time as "the principal's time." In the second case, the teacher views this time as "my time." In the third case, the teacher sees this as "our time" to think, deliberate, and create together.

"No curricular overhaul, no instructional innovation, no change in school organization, no toughening of standards, no rethinking of teacher training or compensation will succeed if students do not come to school interested in, and committed to, learning."
—Laurence Steinberg, author (1996), p. 120

The principal also can frame how teachers, students, and parents relate with the school's physical space. For example, a teacher could walk past a piece of trash in the hallway, believing that keeping the school clean is the custodian's job; he could ignore the trash since it isn't his piece of trash; or he could stop and pick it up out of care for the school. The principal can encourage the latter type of behavior and in general create a greater sense of ownership in the school.

An effective principal promotes healthy collaboration and follow-through without squelching individual initiative and voice. Jim Collins (2001), author of the best-selling business book *Good to Great*, argues that this type of leadership is common at top companies. He notes that strong leaders integrate independent thinking with effective interdependent action:

> Indeed, one of the crucial elements in taking a company from good to great is somewhat paradoxical. You need executives, on the one hand, who argue and debate—sometimes violently—in pursuit of the best answers, yet, on the other hand, who unify fully behind a decision, regardless of parochial interests. (p. 60)

The principal is not the only leader in the school or the only one whose job it is to promote more integrated ways of thinking and acting. This task also falls on the teacher-leaders, parent-leaders, community-leaders, and student-leaders. Ultimately it should fall on all members of the school whose individual actions, taken together, shape the school culture. The school's culture in turn shapes everyone in it. Effective leaders understand and leverage this dynamic.

How to Use the Four Mind-Set Model

As indicated above, school leaders should help move the faculty, students, and parents toward more highly integrated ways of thinking and acting. A good place to start is by helping each school member identify from where along the continuum (from dependent to integrated) they tend to operate. This can be a powerful intervention in itself. The staff also can use the "Rubric of Faculty Interdependence" to more clearly identify the staff's level of independence or interdependence and gain important insights into the relative strengths and weaknesses of their staff culture. (See Resources P, Q, R, and S.)

Many teachers come to realize that they each work, struggle, and succeed on their own and rarely work interdependently with others. This model can expose current limitations, point out new possibilities, and offer specific tools to access more highly integrated ways of working. For example, teachers can learn to collaborate by assessing student work; integrating curricular content and skills across content areas, charting together the high and low points of a school year, deliberately discussing the school's "nondiscussables," and using our "shared agreement protocol."

> "The best gift we receive from great mentors is not their knowledge or their approach to teaching but the sense of self they evoke within us."
> —Parker Palmer, author (1999), p. 19

Shared agreement protocol is a tool to move teachers from independent thinking and individual action to interdependent thinking and collaborative action. (See Resource L.) In working with secondary schools, we often begin by asking the faculty and staff to identify aspects of their daily school culture that interfere with student achievement. For instance, the faculty may identify issues such as student tardiness to class, student use of cell phones, and poor student-teacher relations. Once the faculty selects an issue to work on, then they share their current practices. A teacher in one of our high schools, for example, counted students as tardy if they were not sitting at their desks with their work out when the bell rang. Another teacher only counted students tardy if they showed up fifteen minutes after the bell had rung. Other teachers never took attendance: a clear violation of district policy.

Ultimately the teachers came to a shared agreement about what defined tardiness: a student had to be through the plane of the classroom entrance when the bell stopped ringing to be on time. The teachers also collectively agreed on the consequences for tardiness. Eventually they shared the two written proposals with the students, resulting in additional alterations to some of the consequences. Finally, the faculty gathered to witness each other signing the shared agreement. (In one of our middle schools, the teachers toasted each other with nonalcoholic champagne to celebrate the occasion.)

Then the hard work begins. Teachers read the shared agreement[1] to students every class period for three days. The repeated reading of this policy publicly demonstrates the teachers' commitment to their students to honor the shared agreement. Teachers can begin enforcing the agreement on the fourth day and can track changes in student tardiness by comparing before and after data.

Schools have enjoyed high levels of success through the use of this protocol. In the schools where teachers struggled with student tardiness, some students actually thanked teachers for implementing the effective shared agreement; it was so much easier to go to class since their friends were no longer a magnetic pull to hang out in the empty hallways.

In most schools, policies on tardiness and other expectations are mandated from an administrative level (federal, state, district, principal). Because adherence to these policies requires a simple acceptance or dependent mind-set, many teachers do not readily honor them. Instead they use their personal interpretation. Since independent thinking and action are not working well, we offer an approach that changes a policy mandated from above into a shared agreement among all staff that is created within the scope of the official policy. When all staff participates in its creation and makes a commitment to each other to live by this agreement, the collaboration creates a "policy" that is a living, shared expectation. It is the collective will power that keeps the shared agreement alive!

"The last of human freedoms is to choose one's attitude in any set of circumstances."
                    —Viktor Frankl

If a secondary school has poor student-teacher relations, the faculty might all agree to stand in the doorway of their classrooms and greet each student, every class period of the day. This simple act, occurring thousands of times in a school day, takes little time and money. If done by all teachers as part of a shared agreement, it can transform a school culture. A handful of teachers greeting some students may be of help but it would most likely not have the same power.

Through shared agreements, by collaboratively assessing student work or other such interdependent activities, teachers begin to experience the power of collaboration. The act of developing a shared agreement can build staff confidence and increase the possibility of a school shifting mind-sets.

The Four Mind-Set Model also can reveal how teachers tend to relate to students. One middle school faculty recognized that they kept their students in a state of dependency because they believed that doing so made the teachers' lives easier. They also acknowledged they were probably stifling the students' academic and personal growth in the process; so teachers began gradually shifting from controlling students to fostering greater student self-control. This faculty also realized that since most of the teachers worked out of independent mind-sets, they were reluctant to foster student independent thinking. It appears that teachers who have access to interdependent thinking are more willing to move students from dependence to independence.

Some schools promote more independent and interdependent student thinking and behavior through activities such as daily classroom meetings where student voice is cultivated. This is an especially powerful approach in elementary school settings. In a 15-minute time period, a teacher can elicit student perspectives on the previous school day: What was learned? Were any new ideas introduced? Was the sense of well-being of the classroom community harmed? Was the sense of well-being restored? How do we need to be prepared for today's learning? When this kind of gathering occurs first thing in the morning, it can provide students with an important transition from the previous 18 hours out of school to the six hours of classroom learning.

"The school is the only institution in our nation specifically charged with enculturating the youth into a political democracy."
—John Goodlad, educational researcher and theorist

Some middle schools and high schools achieve these results through effective advisories. Other schools are very good at regular grade-level or all-school meetings. For example, one high school begins its day with all students and faculty gathering in its large foyer. There are student and staff announcements. If a student has been suspended, the student presents a thoughtful apology to the school community, and the community needs to agree to accept the student back. At the end of the 20- to 30-minute gathering, any student or staff member who arrived late apologizes to the community. These schools are not about breaking a rule or about the avoidance of getting caught breaking a rule; they are about taking personal responsibility for the well-being of their school community.

In working with schools that are dealing with complex change, we have found that they need to come to terms with the major components of change such as vision, resources, and action plans and also relate with the "how" of making this happen. In the past, teachers tended to manage change each on their own. For many of today's challenges, teachers need to collaborate to gain the necessary traction for change to occur. The old image of every teacher in his or her own little boat pulling toward his vision needs to be replaced by the image of everyone (staff, students, parents) of a school in the same boat pulling their oars together to make headway toward their shared vision. For example, successful change needs incentives or "what's in it for me," which perhaps now should be thought of as "what's in it for us." For fundamental change to take place, however, many school situations call for its members to have a stake in each other's success. Without this fundamental shift from "me" to "we," successful change just isn't likely.

Overall, the dominant paradigm from which a school community operates constitutes an important aspect of its school culture. Each mind-set has its benefits and liabilities, and simply working harder out of the same mind-set is not enough: schools need to work from more highly integrated mental models. Schools today have maximized their effectiveness from teachers working only out of independent mind-sets. Schools have maximized their effectiveness from students learning only out of dependent thinking and from parents viewing their child's school primarily from dependent or independent perspectives. When a school community—parents, students, and staff—embrace a more integrated way of thinking and acting, it increases its capacity to function at higher levels with a corresponding increase in student achievement and character development.

"America is great because she is good; but if America ever ceases to be good, she will cease to be great."
—Alexis de Tocqueville, French political thinker and historian

Note

1. We adopted the reading of the agreement from Alison Adler, Department of Safe Schools, Palm Beach County School District, Florida.

**RESOURCE K: THE FOUR MIND-SET MODEL: BECOMING MORE
HIGHLY INTEGRATED**

It is not that "dependence" is wrong, it is just limiting. The same is true for independence or interdependence. All three working together—integration—creates three-dimensional space that is very expansive.

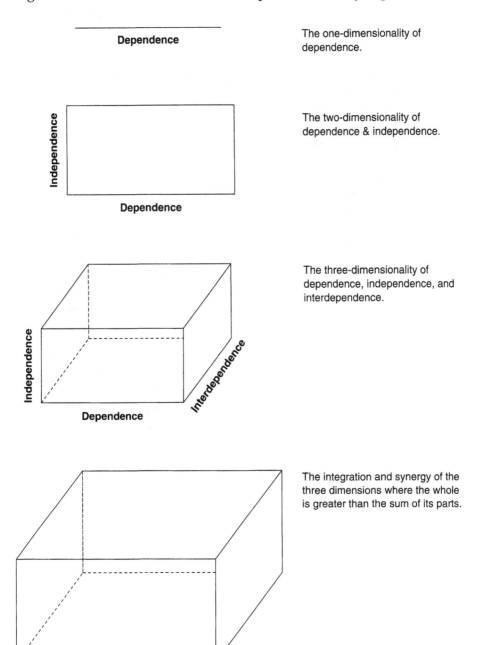

The one-dimensionality of dependence.

The two-dimensionality of dependence & independence.

The three-dimensionality of dependence, independence, and interdependence.

The integration and synergy of the three dimensions where the whole is greater than the sum of its parts.

Integration of dependence, independence, and interdependence

RESOURCE L: USING THE SHARED AGREEMENT PROTOCOL

When faculty and staff work together to create a shared agreement, they develop the power to shape a school culture in which everyone flourishes. A shared agreement encourages adults to work as a team and fosters respect and responsibility among students.

(In schools where the faculty is in agreement with the existing policy, start at Step 6.)

1. **Explain the *shared agreement* philosophy, process, and benefits**—School administrators explain why the school has chosen to create a *shared agreement*. All schools have policies but most faculties do not have shared agreements or ownership of these policies. The process and timeline are explained.

2. **Choose a schoolwide issue**—Faculty votes on one issue such as tardiness, cell phones, or hall passes to develop a *shared agreement* around. Choose a simple issue for your first agreement to build faculty confidence and interdependence. More complex issues such as cheating or agreements about homework are best to address later.

3. **Collect baseline data and set a goal**—Once you choose an issue, identify and/or collect baseline data. Without baseline data, the faculty will not be able to monitor progress (other than anecdotally). Set a goal such as reducing the number of tardies by 40 percent.

4. **Define the *shared agreement* and reach consensus**—First in small groups, then as a large group, teachers reach consensus on the definition of the *shared agreement* (within school district policy). If necessary, teachers also determine consequences as part of the agreement. It is critical that each person supports the agreement fullheartedly.

5. **Solicit feedback**—Ask students for feedback on the *shared agreement*. Consider revising it in light of their feedback.

6. **Commit to the *shared agreement***—Faculty gathers to witness and sign their name to the *shared agreement*, signifying their commitment to each other, their students, and to the school community. This ceremony may include a toast with sparkling cider or the like, marking the importance of this commitment.

7. **Read the script**—Every classroom teacher reads a script of the *shared agreement*, including its consequences, to students every period for two or three days. It is also posted throughout the school.

8. **Implement *shared agreement***—All teachers implement the *shared agreement* following the final day of reading the script. It is essential

that everyone follows it uniformly and consistently. If there is any "grey area," it should be brought to the school leadership as quickly as possible so a decision can be made and publicized.

9. **Review progress, problem solve, and celebrate**—Several weeks after the implementation has started, the faculty meets to share how it is going, address obstacles that have arisen, and celebrate the success. Compare the new data with baseline data to monitor progress. Consider displaying these data in the faculty lounge.

10. **Continue monitoring and renew the commitment to the *shared agreement***—The process is ongoing. Over time, the *shared agreement* becomes a norm that is simply "how we do things here." It becomes part of the school culture. And once a faculty experiences success with one *shared agreement* they can choose to establish the next one. This is how you create an *Intentional School Culture*.

Adapted from Alison Adler, *Single School Culture*, Department of Safe Schools, School District of Palm Beach County, Florida.

RESOURCE M: FACULTY AND STAFF FOUR MIND-SET MODEL

Dependence	Independence	Interdependence	Integration
• I hold a high level of respect for the traditions, rules, policies, procedures, and chain of command of the school.	• I am responsible for teaching, and students are responsible for learning.	• I empathize and care deeply about others and tap into the collective wisdom of the group.	• I recognize the wisdom and the limitations inherent in each paradigm–dependence, independence, and interdependence.
• I readily do what those in charge ask me to do.	• I am self-reliant, inner directed, and I get my needs met through my own efforts.	• I act thoughtfully to facilitate an emerging future where the whole is greater than the sum of its parts.	• I manifest the right combination of those behaviors, be they of a dependent, independent, or interdependent nature, that are most appropriate for each given situation.
• I am directed and sustained by others.	• I take responsibility for doing things efficiently and I work on self-mastery.	• I readily do what is necessary to produce the results that "we" are trying to get.	
• I tend to resist new challenges and to blame others for difficulties.	• I set my own targets and work hard to achieve them.		• I understand that thinking and acting out of one routine and vigorously standing in defense of it, when another mental model is warranted, will result in ineffective action and frustration.
• I usually rely on others to get my needs met, including my sense of self-worth.	• I am unlikely to seek input from others or have a major stake in the success of others.	• I recognize that choosing the right thing to do and how to best do it often comes from the interplay of many people's thinking.	
• I look to others for leadership.	• I focus on doing what I do well, sometimes forgetting to search with others for the most important things on which to focus.	• I access the vast resources of others.	
• At its most enlightened level, this is the wisdom of "not knowing" or humility, which is the ground for all learning.	• I offer fresh ideas and independent action.	• I am not only doing my own work well, I have an active stake in the success of my colleagues.	• I act in ways that are free of habitual patterns, finding the most appropriate response.

RESOURCE N: STUDENT FOUR MIND-SET MODEL

Dependence	Independence	Interdependence	Integration
• I respect the basic expectations and decorum of the school.	• I take responsibility for the grades and behavior needed to achieve particular goals (e.g., get into college).	• I care about becoming a person of knowledge and good character in order to lead a fulfilling life and be of benefit to the lives of others.	• I know when to act in a dependent manner, respecting the given mores.
• I receive information and am able to give back the information to pass tests.	• Learning in itself has limited intrinsic value (e.g., I often copy someone else's homework).	• I accept responsibility for my actions and contribute to the well-being of others (e.g., create a new club to meet a school need).	• I know when to behave independently in a responsible way, and I know when to tap into the collective wisdom and how to skillfully care for the well-being of others.
• I do not hold an abiding commitment to my academic learning and character development.	• I follow rules so that I don't get in trouble.	• I actively contribute to cooperative learning activities.	• I am discerning in knowing the right combination of these wisdoms to use in a given situation.
• I feel that it is important that I don't get caught breaking rules.	• I see teachers in terms of what they can do to help me get what I want.	• I transfer what I have learned across a broad scope of knowledge (e.g., I apply a concept from yesterday's math class to a social issue mentioned in the morning news).	
• I believe that my education is the responsibility of my school (e.g., it is my teacher's fault that I flunked algebra).	• It is not important for me to contribute during cooperative learning activities.	• I protect and defend the rights of others and encourage their growth and development.	
• I tend to focus on me—my desires and my concerns.	• I see school as a zero-sum game (e.g., if someone gets a better grade than I do, it lessens my chances to get into my college of choice).		

RESOURCE O: PARENT FOUR MIND-SET MODEL

Dependence	Independence	Interdependence	Integration
• I respect the traditions, rules, and hierarchy of the school.	• I take responsibility for my child's education and work as a special interest group on behalf of his or her success (e.g., request special academic help, rescue my child from having to take responsibility for his or her actions at school, demand a particular teacher for my child).	• I care about and contribute to the educational experience and well-being of my child and that of all young people.	• I recognize that the best education for my child—as well as that for other children—unfolds through weaving together the insights and energies of parent, child, and teachers and by accessing the appropriate wisdom inherent in the dependent, independent, and interdependent models.
• I drop my child off at school and assume that his or her education is taken care of.		• I understand that educating my child warrants powerful partnerships between home, school, and student where perspectives and pertinent information are readily shared.	• I maximize the wisdom quality of each paradigm and minimize its confused aspects.
• I fill out all required paper work but do not share potentially pertinent information about my child with the school because I view it as family business (e.g., the whole family will be out of the country for two months).	• I see myself exclusively as a client, customer, or consumer of the school.	• I actively seek to establish high levels of communication and trust between home, school, and my child.	
	• I selectively share information pertinent to my child's education with the school.	• I give my child appropriate praise and see his or her school difficulties as opportunities for growth.	
• I do not have specific expectations and requests (e.g., extra challenge in math) for my child's education.	• I feel that our family is in competition with others to get the best out of the school.		

RESOURCE P: USING THE 12 RUBRICS

The 12 rubrics assess a staff's capacity to work interdependently. The instrument includes dimensions such as psychological safety (the degree to which people feel safe voicing opinions, even unpopular ones), the quality of relations with students, and the quality of speech in the school (ranging from gossip to healing language). Staff members are asked to place an X where they think they personally fall along the continuum for each of the 12 dimensions and an O for where they feel the staff as a whole falls. Our office then transposes the X's and O's onto overhead transparencies and analyzes the results with the school.

In the analysis, we look for several things. First, we look to the distribution of X's relative to O's. Typically the X's are higher than the O's, indicating that people see themselves in a better light than they see the staff as a whole. This is particularly true in the area of speech. Apparently what some people view as merely sharing information looks to others like gossip.

Sometimes the discrepancy between X's and O's can reveal something positive. For instance, that the X's are higher than the O's for "morale" can serve to foil attempts by some to convince the rest of the staff that the morale is lousy and that everyone hates working there. (It's hard to maintain this when so many X's are high.) In general, looking at the discrepancy between X's and O's leads to interesting discussions about different perceptions of their school culture as well as each individual's role in it.

It is a good sign when X's and O's line up well, especially if they are clumped in the top two quadrants. This usually indicates that the staff is capable of working at high levels of interdependence. The alignment also might indicate that boundaries between self and others are fluid, perhaps reflecting strong patterns of communication with and empathy toward others.

We also encourage the staff to look at the actual distribution of the X's and O's. A tightly clumped distribution might indicate agreement on an issue (e.g., that morale is relatively high). A wide distribution might indicate that individuals perceive aspects of the school culture in very different ways and that the staff is not in agreement on some issues. Notice the relatively wide distribution of how people perceive trust among the staff in the example school: perceptions range from very low to quite high.

Also notice the outliers in the area of trust. A small group evidently perceives trust to be significantly lower than the rest of the group apparently does. We suggest that a few, or even one, inordinately low dot should not be ignored because they might indicate that a few staff members, who may have a disproportionately strong impact on school culture, see things very differently than the rest. It is often worth exploring this further.

Another benefit of viewing these results publicly is that it allows the staff to draw connections between different aspects of the school culture. For instance, many schools with low psychological safety see a connection with gossip in the school: it makes sense that teachers who do not feel safe sharing concerns publicly will do so privately and feed the rumor mill. One school drew a connection between high professional growth (their commitment to growing and learning as educators) and low morale. They recognized that they were working extremely hard but failing to celebrate either their efforts or their successes, which was taking its toll on morale.

For some schools, this exercise can be a very positive and reassuring activity. It can publicly reaffirm that the staff trust each other, that they feel comfortable speaking up, that relations with students are positive, and that morale is high. We've had at least two schools spontaneously applaud when they saw the results.

More commonly, however, we help a school identify its "weakest link," which prevents it from reaching its full potential. At one school, for instance, the staff came to understand that as a group they are generally resistant to change. This resistance was leading to stress and poor relations between staff and administration, which felt it was their job to carry out district-mandated initiatives. Several other schools realized that as a staff they simply didn't know each other well, and this led to misunderstandings, which fed conflicts.

The apparent remedy, of course, depends on the particular issue, but we work with the staff to identify next steps in addressing an issue. At some schools, we have hired facilitators; at some, we facilitate discussions ourselves; and at others, we have arranged for intensive dialogue groups.

For all schools, we feel that this instrument provides an opportunity to understand their culture more richly and to identify aspects that contribute to its health and aspects that detract from it. The healthier the culture, the more effectively we can teach math and literacy and nurture positive character traits such as respect, compassion, and service.

RESOURCE Q: RUBRIC OF FACULTY INTERDEPENDENCE—TEMPLATE

Instructions: Place an "X" along each of the 12 continua in a spot that you think reflects where you fall individually and an "O" in a spot that reflects where you think the staff falls as a whole. Since each row is a continuum, feel free to place your marks on one side of a box or another or even between boxes. Don't forget to complete both sides! Thank you for your participation.

	Undeveloped	Developing	Developed	Well-Developed
S U P P O R T	Assumes little responsibility for helping meet the needs of others. Is focused on "me" (e.g., is so self-absorbed that there is little awareness of others; grades homework papers in a group meeting).	Assumes some responsibility for the welfare and success of others and the school. Goes along with the group process, but tends to be passive.	Demonstrates a stake in the success of others by supporting their apparent needs. Supports both individuals and the school. Participates and contributes to achieving group goals.	Skillfully supports others through wise, respectful, and timely actions. Has a "we" spirit (e.g., helps mediate a group disagreement; publicly celebrates the success of others). Asks for support when appropriate.
R E L A T E I O N S S H I P W I T H	Teaches a subject and is not interested in the learner. May yell at students and publicly humiliate them. Generally has a poor quality relationship with students. Often expresses negativity and disregard towards young people.	Occasionally helps students with academic issues but is mostly focused on one's own interests. May give attention to some students; this apparent favoritism results in other students feeling rejected. Usually redirects students to seek help elsewhere and may speak to students in a contentious tone.	Enjoys generally positive relationships with students. Students seek out the teacher for academic help and as an adult who will listen to them.	Effectively demonstrates care for all students and helps them learn and fulfill their potential. Is known for being fair, firm, and respectful. Sees the "good" in every young person and knows how to nurture it. Is an advocate for young people and takes judicious risks on their behalf.

(Continued)

RESOURCE Q (Continued)

	Undeveloped	Developing	Developed	Well-Developed
LISTENING	Rarely chooses to listen to others (e.g., never stops talking to listen).	Usually chooses to listen to others but often appears hurried and distracted to speaker.	Listens to others with good understanding, getting the general drift of the conversation (e.g., is preparing one's response while the other person is still speaking).	Listens empathetically and is fully present to the speaker (e.g., makes sure he is really understanding by repeating what he thinks he heard).
COLLECTIVE DECISION MAKING	Resents the collaborative decision-making process and feels that one's own perspective is usually best.	Generally supports the collaborative decision-making process, but may not support the outcome or shared agreements developed by the faculty.	Supports and actively participates in the collaborative decision-making process. Helps the group act on its shared agreements.	Is highly inclusive and constructive during the process of developing and carrying out collective decisions. Helps create the space for these processes to be as healthy and effective as possible.

	Undeveloped	Developing	Developed	Well-Developed
E X P E C T A T I O N S	Has low academic expectations of students and is prone to stereotyping kids as "lazy" or as otherwise unwilling or unable to learn.	Holds fairly low academic expectations for students. Tends to "dumb down" material out of a belief that many students are not capable of more challenging material.	Holds fairly high expectations for students; resists academic stereotyping and uses multiple teaching strategies to reach students with diverse learning styles.	Holds high academic expectations for all students and works hard to draw the most out of every student by accessing and developing their multiple intelligences. Truly sees and develops the potential in every student.
S P E E C H	Often participates in destructive talk (gossip).	Refrains from destructive talk or gossip most of the time (e.g., chooses not to pass on gossip).	Discourages a climate of gossip and promotes accountable talk (e.g., reminds others of the destructive nature of gossip).	Employs speech to heal people and situations. Generally uses speech to support others in the school community and to reach school goals.
R E L A T I O N S	Discounts parents as potential partners in the educational process. Believes that parents should leave the education of their child solely in the hands of the professionals. Feels threatened by some parents and is often reluctant to return parent phone calls.	Views parents primarily as consumers of education, as customers to placate, or as clients who need to be managed. Does not solicit effective partnerships with parents on behalf of students. Interacts with parents as required by the school. May acquiesce to	Understands that the education of children warrants a developmentally effective partnership between home and school.	The teacher pursues effective school, student, and home partnerships through a shared commitment to collaboration, mutual respect, open dialogue, and valuing the parent's perspective regarding the student. Keeps parents

(Continued)

RESOURCE Q (Continued)

	Undeveloped	Developing	Developed	Well-Developed
With PARENTS		the demands of "pushy" parents.	Seeks to establish common goals and maintain effective communication with parents. Keeps parents well informed and seeks their input when appropriate. Offers ways for parents to be involved in the school.	informed through informal and systematic communications. Is aware of parental expectations and aspirations.
TRUST	Feels there is little trust among the staff.	Feels there is some trust among the staff (e.g., faculty occasionally give each other the benefit of the doubt).	In general, feels that the environment among the staff is trusting (e.g., staff often exhibit goodwill towards each other).	Senses among staff a high level of trust (e.g., can count on each other to be honest, just, and reliable).
MORALE	Has low morale. Does not like working in the school (e.g., has poor attendance).	Feels neutral about working here (e.g., "It's not awful, but it's not great").	Likes working in the school and offers suggestions to make things better.	Highly committed and enthusiastic. Takes pride in one's school. Exhibits high morale.
PROF. GROWTH	Is not interested in pursuing professional growth.	Looks to fulfill certification needs with some interest in learning and growing.	Understands one's own strengths and weaknesses and actively pursues professional development in response to student and school needs.	Is a lifelong learner pursuing a wide range of interests and shares areas of expertise with others. Exhibits a high level of professional competence.

	Undeveloped	Developing	Developed	Well-Developed
PSYCHOLOGICAL SAFETY	Often feels afraid to bring up school issues or concerns with the larger faculty and does not feel that he or she has a "voice" at school (e.g., tends to tell others privately after a group meeting what he or she was afraid to bring up at the larger meeting).	Sometimes feels afraid to bring up school issues or concerns with the larger faculty and does not feel that he or she has a "voice" at school (e.g., tends to tell others privately after a group meeting what he or she was afraid to bring up at the larger meeting).	Generally, but not always, feels free to voice opinions at group meetings.	Feels free and open to voice opinions at meetings even if those views might be seen as unpopular. Feels heard.
CHANGE	Highly resistant to and threatened by change (e.g., tends to be negative about any new initiative).	At times can be persuaded to consider new ways of doing things.	Open to embracing new ideas, approaches, and ways of thinking.	Seeks new and more effective ways of reaching goals. Views change as an opportunity.

RESOURCE R: RUBRIC OF POSITIVE INTERDEPENDENCE—FILLED-IN SAMPLE

Rubric of Positive Interdependence for Faculty

Instructions: Place an "X" along each of the 12 continua in a spot that you think reflects where you fall individually and an "O" in a spot that reflects where you think the staff falls as a whole. Since each row is a continuum, feel free to place your marks on one side of a box or another or even between boxes. Don't forget to complete both sides! Thank you for your participation.

	Undeveloped	Developing	Developed	Well-Developed
SUPPORT	Assumes little responsibility for helping meet the needs of others. Is focused on "me" (e.g., is so self-absorbed that there is little awareness of others; grades homework papers in a group meeting).	Assumes some responsibility for the welfare and success of others and the school. Goes along with the group process, but tends to be passive.	Demonstrates a stake in the success of others by supporting their apparent needs. Supports both individuals and the school. Participates and contributes to achieving group goals.	Skillfully supports others through wise, respectful, and timely actions. Has a "we" spirit (e.g., helps mediate a group disagreement; publicly celebrates the success of others). Asks for support when appropriate.
(marks)	O OO	O OOO O OX OX OOO OX OOX OX	X OXO X X OXX XOOX XO XX X	X X XXX X
RELATIONSHIPS WITH STUDENTS	Teaches a subject and is not interested in the learner. May yell at students and publicly humiliate them. Generally has a poor quality relationship with students. Often expresses negativity and disregard towards young people.	Occasionally helps students with academic issues but is mostly focused on one's own interests. May give attention to some students; this apparent favoritism results in other students feeling rejected. Usually redirects students to seek help elsewhere and may speak to students in a contentious tone.	Enjoys generally positive relationships with students. Students seek out the teacher for academic help and as an adult who will listen to them.	Effectively demonstrates care for all students and helps them learn and fulfill their potential. Is known for being fair, firm, and respectful. Sees the "good" in every young person and knows how to nurture it. Is an advocate for young people and takes judicious risks on their behalf.
(marks)	O OO O	O O X OO	OO O X X XX X XXOXXX X X	O X XXO OO XXX O O XO O X

	Undeveloped	Developing	Developed	Well-Developed
L I S T E N I N G	Rarely chooses to listen to others (e.g., never stops talking to listen).	Usually chooses to listen to others but often appears and hurried distracted to speaker.	Listens to others with good understanding, getting the general drift of the conversation (e.g., is preparing one's response while the other person is still speaking).	Listens empathetically and is fully present to the speaker (e.g., makes sure he is really understanding by repeating what he thinks he heard).
C O L L E C T I V E D E C I S I O N - M A K I N G	Resents the collaborative decision-making process and feels that one's own perspective is usually best.	Generally supports the collaborative decision-making process, but may not support the outcome or shared agreements developed by the faculty.	Supports and actively participates in the collaborative decision-making process. Helps the group act on its shared agreements.	Is highly inclusive and constructive during the process of developing and carrying out collective decisions. Helps create the space for these processes to be as healthy and effective as possible.

(Continued)

RESOURCE R (Continued)

	Undeveloped	Developing	Developed	Well-Developed
EXPECTATIONS	Has low academic expectations of students and is prone to stereotyping kids as "lazy" or as otherwise unwilling or unable to learn.	Holds fairly low academic expectations for students. Tends to "dumb down" material out of a belief that many students are not capable of more challenging material.	Holds fairly high expectations for students; resists academic stereotyping and uses multiple teaching strategies to reach students with diverse learning styles.	Holds high academic expectations for all students and works hard to draw the most out of every student by accessing and developing their multiple intelligences. Truly sees and develops the potential in every student.
	O	OO OO O O O X	OO OOOX OO OX XOX OOOX X O X XX X X X XX O XX XX X X	X X O X
SPEECH	Often participates in destructive talk (gossip).	Refrains from destructive talk or gossip most of the time (e.g., chooses not to pass on gossip).	Discourages a climate of gossip and promotes accountable talk (e.g., reminds others of the destructive nature of gossip).	Employs speech to heal people and situations. Generally uses speech to support others in the school community and to reach school goals.
	XX X OO O OOO OO O OOO	OX O X X X O O O O O X OO	XXOX X XX OX X OXX X	X XX
RELATIONS	Discounts parents as potential partners in the educational process. Believes that parents should leave the education of their child solely in the hands of the professionals. Feels threatened by some parents and is often reluctant to return parent phone calls.	Views parents primarily as consumers of education, as customers to placate, or as clients who need to be managed. Does not solicit effective partnerships with parents on behalf of students. Interacts with parents as required by the school May acquiesce to	Understands that the education of children warrants a developmentally effective partnership between home and school.	The teacher pursues effective school, student, and home partnerships through a shared commitment to collaboration, mutual respect, open dialogue, and valuing the parent's perspective regarding the student. Keeps parents

	Undeveloped	Developing	Developed	Well-Developed
With P A R E N T S		the demands of "pushy" parents.	Seeks to establish common goals and maintain effective communication with parents. Keeps parents well informed and seeks their input when appropriate. Offers ways for parents to be involved in the school.	informed through informal and systematic communications. Is aware of parental expectations and aspirations.
	X O / O X / O	O X / O OOO / OX OO / X	X / O X O X OO / OX O XX O X	X / X / O XX / O X X X
T R U S T	Feels there is little trust among the staff.	Feels there is some trust among the staff (e.g., faculty occasionally give each other the benefit of the doubt).	In general, feels that the environment among the staff is trusting (e.g., staff often exhibit goodwill towards each other).	Senses among staff a high level of trust (e.g., can count on each other to be honest, just, and reliable).
	O / OO / X O X	O O X / O O XXX / O X O X X X / XX OO	X / O X O X / X O O X XX / X O O X XX OO	XX X / O X X
M O R A L E	Has low morale. Does not like working in the school (e.g., has poor attendance).	Feels neutral about working here (e.g., "It's not awful, but it's not great").	Likes working in the school and offers suggestions to make things better.	Highly committed and enthusiastic. Takes pride in one's school. Exhibits high morale.
	O X X O / X X OO O / XOXO	X / XO O X X OO O / OOXXXO X X X X	O / O XO / X O XO X / O X X O XO X	XX O / O

(Continued)

RESOURCE R   (Continued)

	Undeveloped	Developing	Developed	Well-Developed
PROF. GROWTH	Is not interested in pursuing professional growth.	Looks to fulfill certification needs with some interest in learning and growing.	Understands one's own strengths and weaknesses and actively pursues professional development in response to student and school needs.	Is a lifelong learner pursuing a wide range of interests and shares areas of expertise with others. Exhibits a high level of professional competence.
	O	X OOOO X OO O O O OO X OO O O OO X OOOXOXXO	XX O X O O OXXOXXOX X	XX X X O X O XXX
PSYCHOLOGICAL SAFETY	Often feels afraid to bring up school issues or concerns with the larger faculty and does not feel that he or she has a "voice" at school (e.g., tends to tell others privately after a group meeting what he or she was afraid to bring up at the larger meeting).	Sometimes feels afraid to bring up school issues or concerns with the larger faculty and does not feel that he or she has a "voice" at school (e.g., tends to tell others privately after a group meeting what he or she was afraid to bring up at the larger meeting).	Generally, but not always, feels free to voice opinions at group meetings.	Feels free and open to voice opinions at meetings even if those views might be seen as unpopular. Feels heard.
	X O X X OO XOO	O X OO OO X OO XX OO X OO	O X O OX O XX O X XO O X O O O X O XX O	X O X X
CHANGE	Highly resistant to and threatened by change (e.g., tends to be negative about any new initiative).	Can at times be persuaded to consider new ways of doing things.	Open to embracing new ideas, approaches, and ways of thinking.	Seeks new and more effective ways of reaching goals. Views change as an opportunity.
	OO	XXX O O OO O XX OX O	XO XO O O X XX X XO O O X XX X OX O X X X	O O X O X X

RESOURCE S: SAMPLE LETTER TO A SCHOOL FACULTY MEMBER REGARDING THE 12 RUBRICS

Dear Faculty:

We at the Office of Character and School Culture applaud your willingness to look carefully at your culture, which is sometimes a painful but always a necessary first step to create a better school. Below we present an analysis of the Rubric of Faculty Interdependence, which your faculty completed on our last visit.

In addition to looking at the absolute values of the X's and O's, we look at their distribution along the continuum, from undeveloped to well-developed. The clustering of points in the middle for support and listening suggests that the staff agree that these areas are satisfactory but could be improved. Staff rated themselves relatively high for generosity, interpersonal, and professional growth. This suggests that staff members are warm and generous with each other and work hard to meet professional goals.

On the other hand, the wider the distribution, the less aligned people tend to be on a particular issue. In your case, the distribution was scattered for the qualities of psychological safety, collective decision making, and morale. Apparently some people feel emotionally safe, can talk to anybody, and are excited to come to work but others feel threatened and don't look forward to coming to work. We wonder how well those on one end of the continuum understand those on the other end.

To find this out, we recommend that you consider forming dialogue groups, each with six to eight faculty members. We are happy to help facilitate them, and you might refer to William Isaacs's *Dialogue: The Art of Thinking Together* for background information on this process (how dialogue differs from discussion, etc.).

Our experience at other schools suggests that when space is created for members of a faculty to listen in a non-judgmental way and understand the perspective of others, tension is reduced and trust is built. This ultimately leads to a more effective school.

Again, we applaud your willingness to explore these issues and to build a healthier school culture. Change theorist Peter Senge said that organizations that take the time to imagine the "future we want to create together" are taking the first step to building success.

Please contact us to talk further about next steps.

Sincerely,
Office of Character and School Culture

THE INTENTIONAL SCHOOL CULTURE

The Eight Gateways

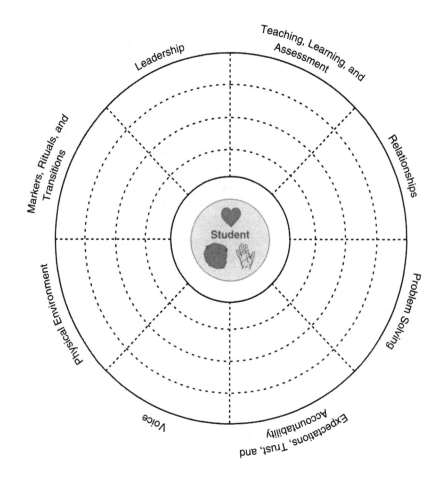

4

Introduction to the Eight Gateways

Y ou have learned about the touchstone and the Four Mind-Set Model. We now introduce the eight gateways, which serve as additional entry points for shaping school culture. It is most useful to turn to the eight gateways once the school has begun addressing the biggest issues facing its culture and has used some of the schoolwide tools discussed earlier in the book.

If you visited three schools and concluded that each had a distinct culture, on what grounds would you base your opinion? You might reply that one school was lackluster while another school was vibrant and nurtured its students. You might notice laughter and openness among staff at one school and distance and chilliness at another. You might hear from some students that school administrators expects much from them academically while elsewhere you might sense that students can skate by. One school might be bright, clean, and inviting; the grounds at another school might be dirty and depressing. At one school, you might hear yelling in the classrooms and a more respectful tone

> "We become teachers for reasons of the heart. But many of us lose heart as time goes by. How can we take heart, alone and together, so we can give heart to our students and our world—which is what good teachers do."
> —Parker Palmer, author (1999)

elsewhere. You might notice that teachers eat lunch alone in their classrooms at one school but eat together elsewhere. These observations provide glimpses into each culture and, taken together, help explain why one differs from another.

The eight gateways are our attempt—after visiting and working with dozens of schools—to create categories for understanding and then shaping school culture. Since you cannot tackle all aspects of your school culture at once, these gateways provide useful entry points. We have included a description of each—in no particular order—including ways to improve it, followed by an assessment tool to determine how strong your school is in each area. You might find that student voice is low at your school or that the staff has concerns about the physical environment. On the other hand, the staff might affirm that academic expectations are high. In any event, this information can steer a staff toward productive ways to improve the school culture.

One school, for instance, determined that the way they typically address problems was a barrier to school improvement. They tended to address issues superficially and failed to get to the root of issues. Unsurprisingly, the issues kept reappearing. This realization led to changing the school schedule to allow for a half-day faculty meeting every other Friday where they could take the time to get to the root of complex issues. This scheduling adjustment has improved both morale and student learning as the staff can now focus more energy on real academic issues.

Gateway 1: Teaching, Learning, and Assessment

Ron Berger (2003) begins his book *An Ethic of Excellence* with a story about his students working diligently for more than three weeks to build a playhouse with their kindergarten buddies. One weekend, while watching the students take great care in spacing the nails, installing clapboard, and painting the trim, he pondered the power and the magic of this work:

> The power of that Sunday was not about New England or playhouse. It was not about gifted kids or clever teaching, or curriculum that should be marketed. There was a spirit, an ethic in the air that day. It was partly about the kids, the teaching, the curriculum, the school conditions, the community, but importantly, it was about all these things at once. It transcended these things. It was the *culture of the school* [italics added] that encouraged these kids to volunteer, to work together, and to care deeply about the quality of what they did. It was the ethic that this school culture instilled. (p. 3)

How do we build such an ethic? How do we instill a sense in our students of what high quality work looks like? It comes from a schoolwide agreement about what counts as good teaching and learning and a commitment to honor that agreement.

Berger, who Harvard Professor Howard Gardner describes as one of the most remarkable teachers in America today, has a few ideas about what some of those agreements ought to be:

- Teachers should meet regularly to discuss student work.
- Students should be allowed to submit multiple drafts of assignments to experience doing high-quality work.
- Students should be shown models of high-quality work as targets before they begin their own work.
- Students should present their work publicly.
- Students should be able to meet state standards through service-learning projects, which tend to engage students.

When teachers agree on high-quality teaching and learning, the results can be powerful. Berger was asked to bring samples of student work, as well as some students themselves, to a meeting in Washington, D.C., with educational policymakers. The adults were astonished at the quality of the students' work. When asked how or why they produced such high quality work, the students were somewhat baffled by the question because high-quality work was all they knew.

Berger freely admits this is the case because all of the teachers in the school shared a common vision and engaged in common practices around teaching and learning. It was not something magical that Berger had done; it was embedded in the culture.

"There are truths that can be told, that knowledge is different from ignorance. Everyone present is expected to be scrupulously truthful in these encounters about what they know or don't know, or more broadly, what they understand or do not understand."
—William Jackson, Robert Boostrom, and David Hansen, authors (1993), p. 19

At many schools, unfortunately, what counts as high-quality teaching and learning is up to each teacher and therefore varies widely throughout the school. Some teachers think students need endless worksheets whereas others might engage students in month-long projects in the community. Even on the mundane level of homework—the quantity and type to assign—many schools lack a shared agreement. Even at the same school some students receive virtually no homework whereas others get a lot; some routinely get busywork, and others get assignments that require much deeper thinking.

Berger notes that there are many places to start when intentionally shaping a school culture, and it will differ at each school. But since his aim is to create "a culture around beautiful student work," he is inclined to begin with student work. This means agreeing on what constitutes high-quality work, which means agreeing on the teaching and learning that will create that work.

At the best schools, teachers not only align the stated curriculum, they also align the hidden curriculum, which itself has enormous power in shaping character.

The *explicit curriculum*, as the name implies, is the actual "stuff" that is taught: fractions, decimals, nouns, the five-paragraph essay, dinosaurs, the Bill of Rights, the presidents, and such. The *hidden curriculum* is everything else in the school that influences children. Harvard's Lawrence Kohlberg made the case in the 1960s and 1970s that the hidden curriculum has more impact than the explicit curriculum. He pointed out that the autocratic nature of many schools, which left students with little voice, had a stronger impact on students' understanding of democracy and power than did the actual social studies lessons about the Bill of Rights. The mismatch between what students learned in class and what they experienced during the day led them to be confused at best or cynical at worst; they were "learning" about democracy but experiencing something very different. As a result, Kohlberg and others established "Just Community Schools" where students democratically participated in the running of their schools.

Another example of mismatch would be a classroom lined with posters promoting "respect" and "kindness" but where the teacher yells at and humiliates students. Again, this will quickly lead to confusion in students, if not anger and cynicism. This may seem an absurd example, but it highlights the importance of aligning the hidden and explicit curriculum of the classroom and the school.

"What makes the assumption of worthwhileness moral is the even more embedded assumption on which it rests, which is that schools and classrooms are places where one goes to receive help, to be made more knowledgeable, and more skillful. Schools and classrooms are designed to be beneficial settings. This implies that the people in charge care about the welfare of those they serve."
—William Jackson, Robert Boostrom, David Hansen, authors (1993), p. 25

The hidden curriculum encompasses the entire school culture and can be seen through all eight gateways, but we focus here on its role in teaching, learning, and assessment. We'll compare two classrooms where the teachers are covering the same explicit curriculum—say, fractions—but imparting a very different hidden curriculum.

The walls of Teacher A's classroom are covered with a variety of posters, including sports figures, one of Miss Piggy stating that "it's not easy being beautiful," and a READ poster featuring Denzel Washington. Teacher A generally greets student questions with a yes or no answer and seems uncomfortable with responses that appear off the mark. She instructs the students to pair up and use the manipulatives as the lesson dictates, but gives little guidance, causing many students to appear confused.

Teacher B covers the same material but in a different way. The visual space in Teacher B's room cues thinking and wondering. For example, a poster of Einstein reads, "Imagination is more important than intelligence," and a handwritten poster states that "the only wrong question is the one you don't ask." In addition, beautiful math projects from previous students hang on the wall, and an "I wonder . . ." board captures student questions throughout the year. Teacher B's tone of voice is positive, and she seems genuinely excited to be sharing the concept of fractions with her students. She responds to questions by asking clarifying questions and by requesting students to verbally articulate how they arrived at an answer, even if it was wrong, because she is interested in their thinking process.

Teacher B encourages novel thinking and often refers to the ways of solving problems as "Jenna's method" or "Kyle's method." She appreciates the connection between discussion and learning and has trained her students to quickly pair up and get to work. In this case, for example, Teacher B models with one of the students what she expects from the student partners. As a policy, she lets students retake quizzes and tests for higher grades, recognizing that students learn at different speeds.

Given the different ways in which the hidden curriculum is enacted, the students in the two classrooms will likely come away from the year with very different lessons. The students in the first classroom can't help but be affected by the lack of enthusiasm with which their teacher delivers the math lessons as well as by her comments about never being very good at math herself. The message is that math is not very fun—and possibly that girls are not good at math. The posters on Teacher A's wall do nothing to inspire learning or suggest the importance of thinking deeply. At best, they are a distraction.

Teacher B communicates very different lessons. The physical environment suggests that thinking and questioning matter. Teacher B's enthusiasm communicates the value of math and mathematical thinking and that women can do it well. The fact that Teacher B ignores harmless distractions in the classroom communicates that her central concern is student learning. Allowing students to retake quizzes and tests reveals that learning is what matters, even if it is a little "late."

One of the central conversations at any school should be ways to identify and support high-quality teaching and learning. Ron Berger notes that creating a culture of quality in his classroom was facilitated by other teachers doing the same in their classrooms—but none could do it on their own. We want schools where teachers agree on what high-quality teaching and learning look like, including what rituals and routines support them and an awareness and commitment to align the hidden curriculum with that vision.

Assessment should be embedded in conversations about teaching and learning; it traditionally has been a tool used to verify learning. An end-of-unit test for instance might verify that students learned the difference between area and perimeter or that they know the basic timeline of events leading up to World War II.

But teachers also can use assessment to enhance learning. Teachers might use short assessments to provide students with mid-unit performance feedback or give them a list of possible end-of-unit questions to focus their learning during the unit. Some schools have trained students to provide constructive feedback to their peers, especially midway through a project. (This is another reason to encourage students to produce multiple drafts of important work.)

Ultimately students should be able to assess their own work and to identify what quality work looks like to verify what they know. Teachers can use assessment as a tool to enhance learning—by providing regular and useful feedback and by providing multiple opportunities to demonstrate mastery, and such—or simply to verify learning. The best schools keep a balance.

Gateway 2: Relationships

Following a violent incident at one of our high schools, we hosted focus groups with students at other high schools in the district. One theme dominated: students thrive in school when they feel cared about by the adults. Students work harder for teachers who care for them, they are less likely to act out when they feel cared for, and they are more likely to show up to school in the first place when they feel at least one teacher cares about them.

These statements are confirmed by numerous studies and by anyone who has spent time with youth. After many months of looking into what works and what does not work at our high schools, including interviewing many students, the Denver Public Schools Commission on Secondary Education concluded much the same thing: that students need the three R's from school—relationship, rigor, and relevance.

> "No significant learning occurs without a significant relationship."
> —James Comer,
> Yale psychiatrist (2004)

Too many students do not feel cared about in our schools but not necessarily because their teachers do not care about them. Most teachers care for their students. However, students do not always receive these messages of care. We saw this at one middle school we visited. When the school asked its students to write down the number of adults at school who they thought cared for them as human beings, the teachers were stunned by the number of students who felt that only one of their teachers cared about them and by the number of students who felt that no one cared. We recommended that the school interview students to learn what made them feel cared for.

A longitudinal study involving nearly 400 middle school students asked this question and came up with the following results. Students perceive that teachers care about them when teachers:

1. Model caring and show that they care about teaching by making class interesting

2. Engage in democratic interactions, such as listening openly and paying attention to student questions and needs, keeping promises, and trusting students

3. Show regard for all students' individual learning needs and contributions as well as for their nonacademic situation, such as by explaining lessons in multiple ways and taking a personal interest in them (e.g., asking how their weekend was)

4. Offer nurturing feedback, such as praise on work done well or an expectation that future work will rise to the student's true ability

The study found that perceived caring from teachers was "significantly and positively" related to students' pursuit of prosocial goals and academic effort (Wentzel, 1997). It confirms what many of us see every day: that students work hard for teachers with whom they connect.

Class meetings are a good way to build caring relationships, especially at the elementary level. These gatherings go by various names, such as "circle time," "community gathering," or "morning meeting," and generally take between 15 to 20 minutes per day. They are a space where students and their teacher share with each other, learn from each other, and develop trust within the group. Many teachers prime the academic day with activities during the meeting, such as group skip counting. Schools that have implemented these regular gatherings have noticed big changes not only in the culture of individual classrooms (especially with how students work together on assignments and projects) but in the culture of the school as a whole.

We spoke with one teacher who decided not to do circle time one year, believing that she did not have time for it. Since she noticed such a difference in how students treated each other and in the number of classroom disruptions compared to previous years, she reintroduced it the following year. Schools tend to notice the biggest effects from these gatherings after the first year, when students (and teachers) are more familiar with the ritual.

At the secondary level, advisory groups can have the same bonding effect as morning gatherings. Advisory can become a home base for students and a place where they can get to know students outside of their social group. Also, because students are more likely to feel disconnected in a large middle school or high school than in an elementary school, a strong relationship with an adult adviser—especially one who acts as an advocate—can mean the difference between a student flourishing or dropping out of school.

In general, how do students treat each other in your school? If bullying is a problem, students may not feel emotionally safe enough to concentrate on their learning. On the other hand, norms of kindness can enhance learning. At some schools, older students read to their younger "buddies," new students are inducted into the school by veteran students, and better-performing students tutor those who need a little more time.

Relations among adults also impact school culture and can influence student performance. As mentioned earlier, numerous studies, including Byrk and Schneider's *Trust in Schools* (2002), validate the connection between relational trust and increased student performance. Teachers go that extra mile for each other and for their kids in an atmosphere of trust.

On the other hand, students easily pick up on and are often negatively impacted by discord among staff.

One alternative high school noticed that the students who dropped out tended to be those without strong relationships to staff members. Therefore they devised an interesting survey for students. In one column, students checked the names of staff members with whom they were at least acquainted. In the second column, they checked the names of staff members with whom they would feel comfortable sharing something important about their life. The school created a list of students with zero or one name checked in the second column. The list included approximately 30 names. The school gave teachers a list of students who had checked their name in the second column and bolded the names of those students where that teacher was the only named checked. Many teachers were surprised by who was on their list, often not realizing how important their connection was to that student.

The staff then discussed strategies—some of them very simple—to try to connect to those thirty students and even to enhance relations with those on their individual lists. The school set a goal of cutting the list of 30 students in half after two months, at which time the school would survey the students again. The school exceeded their goal, cutting the list to just ten names. This focused attention on strengthening relationships will undoubtedly have an impact on the school's dropout rate.

Another topic relevant to relationships—but not often talked about in the field of education—is forgiveness. An occupational hazard of teaching is the high likelihood of being hurt, sometimes deeply, by those you teach or even by your fellow teachers. We recently met an award-winning teacher from Wisconsin at a conference who shared a story about his professional life. Several years earlier, he attended a graduation party to present a gift to some of his students. One of the other students—not one of his own—made a lewd gesture at him in front of the other guests. Feeling humiliated, the teacher wrote this student a letter over the summer, expressing his displeasure at the student's actions. The teacher then dropped the issue and tried to forget about it. Three years later, the student came back to school to visit some friends. After merely seeing the student down the hall, the teacher said his face turned red and his chest tightened as if the offense had just happened the day before. The teacher thought he had dealt with his feelings but apparently had just buried them.

One wonders how much space this anger had been taking up in the teacher's heart over the last three years. Odds are this was just one of

"We noted several attributes of interpersonal relations in the schools that were associated with effective programs or periods of program effectiveness. Students felt cared about and respected, teachers shared a vision and sense of purpose, teachers and students maintained free and open communication, and all parties shared a deep sense of trust."

—Robert Rossi and Samuel Stringfield, authors (1997), p. 3

many hurts the teacher had sustained during that time. At some point if the teacher continues to bury those feelings of anger and resentment, it likely will begin to affect how the teacher relates to other students and to his job in general.

We have met other teachers who harbor deep resentment toward a principal or another colleague many years after an event. We know one teacher who is so angry at "the district"—10 years after an event—that the teacher shakes when he speaks about it.

Forgiveness is only one way to deal with resentment, but it is sometimes the most effective. Robert Enright (2001), author of *Forgiveness Is a Choice,* validates the anger and resentment we feel after being hurt unjustly but argues that hanging on to it too long ends up harming the victim even more and prevents us from flourishing. It saps our energy and sometimes changes our worldview. In the case of teaching, it could change our view of students in general. In his book, Enright proposes steps to take to work through deep anger held toward a friend, a colleague, or even a student from five years ago. The relationship between teachers and students can help mediate the teaching and learning process; we need all the tools we can find to make these relationships as healthy as possible.

Although forgiveness should never be forced (nor should apologies—something many of us are guilty of, especially with younger children), it is a skill worth discussing with our students as well. Children seem naturally good at forgiving—a best friend can be forgiven even before lunch recess ends—but many gradually join adults in the practice of clinging unprofitably to resentment.

Relations with parents also help define the quality of a school's culture. Parents who feel welcomed by and connected to the school are more likely to support school activities and partner with teachers in the academic and social development of their child. On the other hand, parents who feel intimidated or otherwise not welcomed will rarely come through the front door.

The quality of relationships is a salient aspect of a school culture. It is worth assessing whether the relationships serve as a resource in your school or whether they work against it.

Gateway 3: Problem Solving

How a school faces challenges speaks volumes about its culture. Some schools address problems head-on and by their root causes whereas others let them fester or treat only the symptoms. For instance, a teacher may deal effectively with an incident of cheating in his or her class but fail to recognize that the student has been cheating for many years and in many classes. In a sense, the problem has not been solved and will surely return.

It could be otherwise. A big reason that schools fail to get to the root of issues is because teachers deal with the issues individually instead of as an entire staff. Consider the example of cheating. A school of 30 teachers could have 30 ways of approaching cheating, or it could approach it as a staff. If teachers take the latter approach, they have a much better chance of identifying systemic issues that contribute to the problem as well as identifying repeat offenders. After looking into it, they may find that cheating happens most often in certain types of classes or with certain types of assignments. They may decide on a schoolwide policy that includes ways to detect cheating, to reduce it, to treat first and second offenses, and so on. A staff may gain more insight from focus groups into why students cheat in the first place. They may find that skill deficits—and not exclusively lack of ethics—contribute to the problem. Afterschool math tutoring may be what some of these offenders really need.

Student behavior is another good example. Imagine how many student referrals and classroom disruptions could be eliminated if we could get to the root issues behind the problems even if we did so with only a few kids. (Surely the 90/10 rule applies to discipline issues where 90 percent of referrals and disruptions come from 10 percent of our kids.) This would take an initial investment of time—root causes are rarely easy to discern—but the rewards can be huge. Schools that have adopted a schoolwide discipline plan and held to it have reaped huge benefits for both staff and students. Educator Ruth Charney (2002) notes that any effective discipline plan needs to create both self-control and community; otherwise schools will only be treating symptoms. In addition, an increasing number of schools have adopted variations of restorative discipline—an approach that aims to repair harm instead of merely punish—and is more likely to get at root issues. But again, this requires commitment from the entire staff.

> "Top drawer teaching and learning can never flourish in a sterile or toxic environment."
> —Terrance Deal and Kent Peterson, authors (1999), p. 11

Unfortunately, for a variety of reasons including limited time, few schools function this way; they go on treating issues one episode at a time, one classroom at a time. This is why issues such as tardiness, cheating, and bullying persist.

At some schools the principal tries to solve all the problems, while other schools address problems collectively. Principals who try to handle it all have all kinds of reasons for doing so: Teachers are too busy and don't want to be bothered. It takes too much time to get input. It's my job as a principal to make decisions, and so on. Whatever the reasons, these principals forego the benefits that different perspectives bring to problem solving. Sometimes if a problem is framed differently—which is more likely when more than one person is looking at it—it is much easier to address.

Some schools solicit help from students to solve problems. A good example comes from an elementary school in Denver. About seven years ago the physical education teacher, Chris Baumgartner, decided to ask her older students to help address issues on the playground. The result is her hugely successful P.E.Aces (a play on the word "peace") program. The P.E.Aces, who are fourth and fifth graders, each host a "station" at recess. Working often in pairs, they host a basketball station, a jump rope station, a "shark attack" station, or any of the many other recess games, all of which have been taught in a physical education class. The P.E.Aces are there to help to reinforce skills, to reteach rules, and to help settle any disagreements among participants. They can even join in the games if they want. Many younger students look up to them and someday may fill their shoes.

The results of the program have been amazing. Almost all playground fights have been eliminated, and students are returning to class in a better mind-set to learn. In addition, relations have improved between older and younger students, older students are developing real responsibility, and the school had not lost a single piece of sports equipment in the last five years. Other teachers feel it has had a positive effect on the entire school culture.

"The way we diagnose our students' condition will determine the pedagogical 'prescription' we offer. Rather than rely on stereotypical interpretations of student behavior, we need to understand their marginality and decode the fears that often drive their lives."

—Parker Palmer, author
in Livesey & Palmer (1999), p. 21

In another district, the districtwide student board has partnered with the school board and superintendent to try to improve district pride by communicating to fellow students the importance of the annual state-mandated assessment (where schools are ranked by the state). The students recognized that some of their friends did not take the tests seriously, even filling in patterns on the answer sheet instead of taking time to actually answer the questions. After seeing the link between low scores, reputation of the district, student enrollment, and district budget, the student board members are engaging in a campaign to raise test scores and therefore increase pride.

For a school or district to encourage students to help address issues and solve problems, it must first see students as potential resources instead of as merely objects of instruction. We talk more about this subject in the "Voice" section in this chapter.

The mental mind-sets dominant at a school can impact how its members solve problems. At many middle schools and high schools, the dominant mind-set among teachers is independence; that is, close the door and do your own thing. This mind-set creates problems such as widely uneven enforcement of even a very clear tardy policy. Some teachers record all students who are not in their seat right as the bell rings while others do not care if students arrive five minutes late. A different mind-set will be needed to solve this problem. Albert Einstein wrote, "Major problems cannot be solved at the same level of thinking that created them." Asking each teacher to develop his or her own solution will only exacerbate the problem. What is needed is a solution based on interdependence. The teachers need to collectively agree on a strategy and then collectively agree to follow it. They must realize that their actions—in this case, the degree to which they enforce the tardy policy—affect the other teachers throughout the school and therefore the larger school culture. Teachers also need to help students recognize that arriving late to class not only affects their learning but that of others as well.

School faculties should try to solve problems like these early, before they develop into bigger ones. One effective strategy is to use the School Culture Survey at regular intervals even when no obvious crisis is present. We visited several schools that had a very difficult year (and eventually a change in leadership) partly because they lacked a system to detect early signs of trouble. From these experiences, we developed the School Culture Survey to determine whether the staff feels the school is heading in the right direction, whether they are on the same page, whether there is healthy communication with the administration, and whether things tend to get done at the school. A critical, open-ended final question asks which action each would take to improve the school. We believe that all schools can benefit from such a tool but especially those with new leadership. We administer the surveys online using www.Survey Monkey.com (there are many similar services available), which makes collecting and analyzing the data easy. (See Resource A at the end of Chapter 1 for this survey.)

"A child is a person who is going to carry on whatever you have started. He is going to sit where you are sitting and when you are gone, attend those things which you think are important. You may adopt all the policies you please, but how they will be carried out depends on him. He will assume control of your cities, states and nations. He's going to move in and take over your churches, schools, universities and corporations. Your books are going to be judged, accepted or condemned by him. The fate of humanity is in his hands. So it might be well to pay him some attention."

—Abraham Lincoln

The School Culture Survey can also help identify the "nondiscussables," if there are any at your school. It is amazing how long these elephants can live right in the middle of the living room before they are named and addressed. And usually the longer they are there, the greater the (usually negative) impact on school culture and on student learning. Race is the nondiscussable at some schools. At others, it is ineffective leadership. Is there something comparable at your school?

Schools need effective problem-solving tools and methods to operate in the face of persistent change. Conditions change throughout our lives; we must prepare our students for these changes. One of the authors (Charles Elbot) of this book was born in 1947 and has experienced in these years a range of cultural perspectives. In the years since then, schools have transitioned from being concerned with whether John was chewing gum in class to whether John was carrying a weapon.

In the 1950s, Elbot lived in a somewhat simplistic world of black and white conventional thinking where his country and its leaders, whether right or wrong, were right! He believed in unquestioning patriotism and the societal status quo. The integrity of the president of the United States was never in question. But the civil rights movement and the anti-Vietnam War protests of the 1960s changed everything. He no longer held to a sole unifying set of beliefs. Everything was questioned to the point where it seemed that few foundational practices like respect and responsibility remained.

In partial response to this period, the 1970s brought us the notion of values clarification. This belief held that all values were equal and no one's values could be imposed on another. The challenge was only to be clear about one's own beliefs. Thus we entered an era of moral relativism where almost everything was permissible.

Elbot learned that blind obedience to authority is dangerous, yet critical inquiry in the absence of universal values such as respect leads to a self-centeredness and contempt for the rights and well-being of others. He learned that society transmits a seemingly coherent ethical view until that approach collapses under its inability to come to terms with the given challenges. As educators, we would do well to remember that the world we are preparing our students for may look very different than the one today, and the tools we have used to address issues in the past may need to be replaced with other tools in the future.

It is worth asking how challenges are addressed in your school. Are they swept under the rug? Are they dealt with at the root level? Are multiple perspectives invited? Do you have structures to provide early signs of trouble? Are you constantly adapting your tools to address the new challenges facing our schools and society?

Gateway 4: Expectations, Trust, and Accountability

Expectations are like magnets: they can either pull students and staff up or pull them down. But high expectations are not enough—support, trust, and accountability are also needed.

Students and staff quickly figure out what is expected of them. At some schools and in some classes, students know they have to stretch. We all remember the tough teacher who pushed us and for whom we always made sure we completed our homework with care. But we also remember those teachers whose classes were fun but where we hardly learned anything, those teachers who were strict and expected our best behavior, and those teachers who put up with almost any kind of behavior from students. Some teachers—perhaps the ones we remember most—expected special things from us: to be curious, to explore new ideas, to develop a sense of humor. The most effective schools communicate high expectations in all aspects of the school.

One of the best ways to do this is with the school touchstone. The school touchstone should communicate the core academic and ethical qualities that your school stands for. The Slavens Code of Conduct, for example, begins by announcing: "At Slavens we take the high road." It unambiguously communicates that the school expects your best at all times. The statement continues by describing what doing your best might look like: "We show and receive respect by using kind words and actions, listening thoughtfully, standing up for ourselves and others, and taking responsibility for our own behavior and learning." The final line reminds us to be accountable: "This is who we are even when no one is watching!"

> "With increasing frequency these days, teachers are evaluated on the basis of how successful they are in getting their students' test scores to rise. Perhaps a more fundamental criterion would be to look at how helpful teachers are as members of the school community in providing leadership that will improve the culture of the school and make it hospitable to everyone's learning. For, as we know, more than anything else it is the culture of the school that determines the achievement of teacher and student alike."
> —Roland Barth, author (2001), p. 78

At Bromwell Elementary, the BEAC Way—Bromwell Eagles Always Care—also communicates high ethical standards. This simple statement leaves little doubt that care and compassion are expected from students, staff, and parents.

The Greenwood Creed from Greenwood Elementary communicates the importance of respect and responsibility and also of stretching your mind: "We pursue learning with eagerness. We challenge ourselves intellectually." Greenwood's expectations are clear.

Teachers at another school expect students to turn in multiple drafts of writing and to critique each other's work through regular peer-editing sessions. This is true for stories, book reports, and even for thank-you notes to class visitors. The expectation is for students to keep working on something until it is of high quality. This expectation holds for all types of work, including art projects and even spelling tests.

But high expectations are not enough. We must combine support, trust, and accountability with these expectations. For example, Slavens School supports its students' efforts to take the high road by identifying what "taking the high road" looks like. Teachers pause while reading books and ask if a character in the story is taking the high road, they discuss figures in history who took the high road, and they discuss how difficult and unpopular it can be to take the high road. Slavens gives its students the opportunity to write about times when they have taken the high road—and times when they have not. Teachers at Slavens have made "taking the high road" part of the school's lexicon and therefore support students in making it a way of life.

Bromwell Elementary gives its students opportunities to care by joining multigrade, service-learning teams that meet throughout the year, among other things. Last year these teams raised money for UNICEF as part of the "Kids Helping Kids" campaign. In addition, teachers regularly highlight themes of caring and compassion in lessons and in classroom behavior, thus reinforcing their importance.

As mentioned earlier, a growing number of schools use rubrics to hold students accountable for honoring the touchstone. These rubrics, which can take the form of small booklets, help clarify what behaviors reflect qualities in the touchstone. Without them, words like "respect" and "responsibility" can seem vague to both students and teachers.

Consider how Rosedale Elementary clarifies what "responsibility" looks like. Behaviors that the school deems unsatisfactory include failing to complete and return homework, losing things, not following teachers' directions, and routinely blaming others for his or her behavior. On the other hand, behaviors that the school considers developed in this area include completing and returning homework, regularly following teachers' instructions (even when no one is watching), and owning up to his or her own behavior.

The rubric sheet includes strategies for teachers to develop responsibility in students. These strategies include giving positive feedback for completing assignments and for following school rules along with creating a classroom job chart for classroom responsibilities. Teachers ask students to commit to several strategies of their own to develop in each area.

Ideally these rubrics should follow students throughout their school careers and should chart growth in key character areas (both academically and ethically). Teachers should meet briefly with each student to provide feedback and set goals and should revisit with students later in the year. Rubrics provide support and accountability in many ways: They help clarify what these traits look like (and don't look like), provide strategies to both teachers and students for how to develop them, and provide a way of measuring student progress.

But what about maintaining high expectations for teachers? One high school has taken a unique approach; one that we feel will be widespread in the field soon.

The staff in this high school spent a retreat weekend developing five core agreements that defined what it meant to be a productive member of the school. They believed that the school could reach its highest potential if all staff members met or exceeded expectations in all these areas. The agreements ranged from being a good team player to developing expertise in their field, and the staff developed rubrics for each agreement clearly stating what it meant to exceed, meet, or not meet expectations. Each spring the staff, including the custodian and the principal, anonymously provide feedback to fellow staff members on how well they uphold the agreements. They leave areas blank where they lack information to provide meaningful feedback. For instance, the 10th-grade history teacher might leave the academic expertise section blank for the chemistry teacher if he or she has never seen the chemistry teacher teach.

"You must . . . have the discipline to confront the most brutal facts of your current reality, whatever they may be."
—Jim Collins, author (2001), p. 13

Staff members receive their own Staff Reflection Tool (as the process is known) with feedback from colleagues. School administrators encourage staff members to process this feedback with a trusted peer and remind them to look at patterns not necessarily individual marks. No one in the administration sees the results; it is simply feedback from which each individual can learn and grow. One principal was taken aback at first when she learned that several staff members gave feedback that she was treating them with less respect than before:

> But after I thought about it some, I realized that I had been "on the run" and that I was cutting people off in mid-sentence. The last thing I wanted to do was show disrespect to my wonderful staff. I am glad that I got this feedback so I could have the opportunity to change. Also, most of the feedback I got was really affirming, which made me feel good.

There is much to recommend about the staff reflection process. First, it defines clearly what is expected from teachers; no more guessing what it means to be a great teacher at a particular school. Second, it is democratic. It is one of the few times that a custodian has as much "power" as a principal. Third, it leverages the positive power of peers. Many teachers value the professional opinions of their colleagues more than those of the administration. Therefore this feedback carries substantial weight. This works for both positive and negative feedback. Staff members often feel enormously affirmed by feedback from their peers—sometimes more so than from vague praise by the principal.

This process also helps break what we call the "yeller syndrome." Some schools have a teacher who regularly yells at students or otherwise engages in unprofessional behavior, but no one on staff either sees it as their job or is otherwise willing to confront this teacher. Yes, this may be the principal's job but for a variety of reasons sometimes no action is taken. So the yeller continues to yell for years without being confronted or given support to develop new skills. Peer reflection can address this. It would be hard for this teacher to ignore when half the staff rates him as not meeting expectations for how he or she relates to students.

There are other ways for staff members to hold each other accountable. One school chose to develop their "five agreements" beginning with a self-evaluation before launching into a staff evaluation. Whatever the method in this era of high accountability, schools must find ways to maintain high professional standards across the entire staff. Ultimately all staff members—from the custodian to the third-grade teacher to the principal—are in the same boat and need to recognize that each person's actions affects the whole team.

Staff members will more likely grow professionally in an atmosphere of trust. Growing requires taking risks, and we are much more likely to do this when we trust and have faith in those around us. This is a crucial point to remember about students as well; students grow the most when they trust their teachers, the school, and the system.

A brief story illustrates this point. Years ago, we went on a 10-day Outward Bound trip with other educators. Our leader, Allie, had led wilderness trips for years and was an experienced rock climber. She led the hikes, but on about Day 4 she told us that she would be hanging back and that we should go ahead without her. (It turns out that we were always in her view, but this was not always apparent to us.) Many of us saw the Outward Bound philosophy at work: facilitating growth by taking people out of their comfort zone. We trusted this was good for us, and we went along with it. We also trusted Allie—both that she had our best interests at heart and that she was competent. This trust was crucial for our willingness to grow—and grow we did. We forded rivers, hiked steep mountains, and frequently went out of our comfort zone.

But not everyone on the trip had the same trust in Allie or apparently in the whole enterprise—at least initially. One person tried to lead a revolt when Allie "abandoned" us on Day 4, and she started heading back to the trailhead (until we talked her out of this). Others similarly were hesitant to continue the hike.

By the end of the trip, we all were willing to step out of our comfort zones, and we all grew immensely from the experience. But the difference early on—why some of us embraced the challenges immediately and others resisted—had to do with trust. Once we established and felt trust, we all grew.

Think about the connections between trust and schooling. Even with high expectations, support, and accountability, student growth may be stifled without trust. Just as on our Outward Bound trip, students need to be able to trust that their teachers are competent and have their best interest at heart. Students who trust their teachers will take risks and be open to the type of feedback and candor from their teachers that they might not be open to otherwise. And this feedback may be just what they need to grow.

"The culture, and we as members of it, have yielded too easily to what is doable and practical. . . .We have sacrificed the pursuit of what is in our hearts. We find ourselves giving in to doubts and settling for what we know how to do, or can learn to do, instead of pursuing what matters most to us and living with the adventure and anxiety that this requires."
—Peter Block, author (2003), p. 1

Not all students need a highly trusting relationship with a teacher to thrive: some simply want a competent algebra teacher. And not all students need teachers to hold them accountable for doing work well: they may already be driven by a strong sense of internal accountability. The best teachers help students thrive by matching their particular mixture of needs for a trusting relationship, high expectations, and accountability.

Gateway 5: Voice

Voice reflects how much one feels "heard" at school. Students who are heard by teachers and administration feel more connected to their school and more invested in their own learning. Unfortunately, many students report feeling like "passengers" in their school.

What do we mean by student voice? It comes in many forms, but the effect is the same: more student engagement and a greater connectedness to school. At one school, student voice is reflected in a strong peer mediation program. Instead of having the adults try to solve everything, these mediators have shown how effective students can be at addressing behavioral issues. The school wisely invited a broad range of students to join the group, giving it wide credibility among students. A character education club at another school has taken this even one step further: the majority of its members are from some of the "toughest" crowds in the school. The adult advisor feels that if she can empower this group of students, they can help turn the school around.

Student voice can be seen within individual classrooms. When appropriate, teachers can give students a choice of a topic for projects or research assignments. Some English teachers, for example, give students choices about the books they read. The more choice and voice a student feels in academic classes, the more engaged they are likely to become.

Student voice also is visible in more subtle ways within classrooms. One way is how teachers respond to students' answers and comments: they can either invite voice or shut it down. Some teachers effectively shut children down if they do not produce the exact answer the teachers are fishing for. On the other hand, other teachers probe deeper into why a student answered a certain way with a comment such as, "That's interesting, tell me what led you to that conclusion?" or "That's creative, tell me more." In such settings, it is clear that teachers welcome a student's *academic* voice.

In fact, not nurturing some degree of student voice may be one of the surest ways to disengage students, which can lead to low academic achievement and behavior problems. Students who feel powerless and see little prospect of expressing power through official channels are more likely to act out in inappropriate ways. We met with one student who was in the principal's office for using the faculty men's room instead of the student bathroom. When asked why, the student replied that the regular bathroom did not have stall doors. Always seen as a "bad kid," the student felt little confidence in getting the ear of someone who could have doors put on.

Focus groups reveal that students share a similar sentiment about a desire for appropriate voice. Students want to be listened to; they feel they have important things to say, but do not feel there are structures in place or an overall commitment to listen to them. When adults stifle student voice, they lose a potentially important ally because students and teachers ultimately want the same thing: a better school.

This is particularly true with school safety. A typical high school might have 100 adults and 1,200 students. Those 1,200 students can either be allies for school safety (keeping an eye out for weapons, notifying teachers about an upcoming fight, etc.) or bystanders or even adversaries. The adults cannot do everything alone.

On a more positive note, schools can leverage student voice to partner with students in raising test scores and improving learning. Imagine if a youth council at your school took on the challenge of improving math scores—they might have some terrific ideas.

"We don't know who we are until we hear ourselves speaking the drama of our lives to someone we trust to listen with an open mind and heart."
—Sam Keen, American author, professor, and philosopher

Nurturing appropriate levels of student voice does not mean pandering to students. For instance, students should not get to vote whether they have to take math or whether they have to show up to school on time. Voice comes with responsibility: responsibility to make good decisions and responsibility to follow through. Unfortunately, more schools are on the other end of the spectrum: they nurture too little student voice. And the cost is high not just in terms of the functioning of the school but also in terms of the development of those students.

One of the best ways to engage student voice is through service learning. Service learning is a teaching strategy that combines gaining academic skills and knowledge with addressing a real community need. Often there is space for students to have a choice of project or at least choices *within* the project. For instance, students might learn about World War II or the Vietnam War by interviewing veterans and then writing a booklet or creating a short video based on their stories. Students in several local elementary schools met the state standard of writing a persuasive letter by writing letters to high school seniors encouraging them to vote and enclosing a blank registration form. The letters were heartfelt and compelling and probably increased the likelihood that both the senior and fifth grader will become lifelong voters. Second graders at another school learned about the body and improved their reading, writing, and public speaking skills by organizing an antismoking campaign in their school and

"It is individuals and small groups of teachers and principals who must create the school and professional culture they want. This is what's worth fighting for—inside and outside your school."
—Michael Fullan and Andy Hargreaves, authors (1996), p. 107

surrounding neighborhood. The teacher said that in her 20 years of teaching she had never seen children so engaged in their learning: "When they were reading books to prepare for their presentation, they did not even realize that they were reading!"

Teacher voice and parent voice are also important. As with students, when teachers and parents feel heard, they feel more ownership in the success of the school. We measure the degree of psychological safety teachers feel at school relative to how comfortable they feel voicing their views at school, particularly at faculty meetings. This measurement is a proxy for teacher voice, and we find a strong correlation between high psychological safety and a high-performing school. It makes sense: teachers thrive and feel more ownership in their school when they feel others listen to them.

This is also true for parents. Does your school invite parents to join school committees? Does your school include parents in the shaping of the school mission statement or school touchstone? The degree to which parents feel welcomed by a school can help determine how much voice they will eventually feel and therefore how much they will contribute to the school.

Gateway 6: Physical Environment

The physical environment is the container that holds all other parts of the school and can impact how people feel about being part of your school. It is also one of the first things people notice about your school. It should be safe and clean, inviting and inspiring, and conducive to learning. Also consider how the environment around your school grounds can support your school's mission and vision.

In *Savage Inequalities: Children in America's Schools,* Jonathan Kozol (1991) famously documented the way the physical environment of schools impacts how students feel about themselves and their learning. Students at one inner-city school had to use umbrellas when going to some classrooms because the roof leaked so badly. Kozol reported that these students felt devalued compared to students across town who were treated to state-of-the art learning and athletic facilities. Of course poor districts may not be able to afford the best facilities, but there are small things schools can do to improve their physical environment to make staff, students, and parents feel welcome.

For instance, does the entrance of your school feel inviting? Are there comfortable tables and chairs for visitors? Du Bois Middle School had a drab entranceway until a parent donated two couches, an area rug, and a glass coffee table. Together with three plants purchased by the school, the space feels very different now and is much more inviting to visitors than the hard benches in the main office.

Is the school clean? Trash on the school grounds might send the message that "these people don't care" and can prefigure the unraveling of other aspects of your culture. We are well to keep in mind the "broken glass" theory here: taking care of the small stuff can prevent bigger issues from developing. This applies to cities as well as to schools.

Does the library make you feel like pulling a book off the shelf and start reading or does it feel like you have entered a doctor's office? Are there soft chairs to sit on and fun nooks and crannies that beckon young readers? Some libraries become the center of school activity, whereas others are almost always empty.

How classroom teachers arrange furniture in their classrooms and displays on the walls also matters. Tables or desks arranged in pods communicate that collaboration is valued; whereas desks bolted down in rows from classrooms of old communicate just the opposite. It might be worth having a colleague take a look at your room to offer suggestions. A math classroom at one high school has mathematical formulas—and a few jokes—on posters painted by former students plastered all over the walls. The physical environment there sends the unmistakable message that this is a mathematically serious (but also fun) place and one where student voice matters.

A teacher at Oakland Elementary displays pictures of and quotations from heroes such as Gandhi, Nelson Mandela, and Martin Luther King, Jr., in the hall along with traits such as honesty, love, compassion, and kindness. She also posts questions for passers-by on which to reflect: Have you been kind today? Who did you help today? Have you done your best? What is on the wall not only will inspire you, it will engage you in conversation.

Lighting matters. One school exchanged its harsh florescent light tubes with soft, warm, sunlight-like lighting that changed the feel of the school. The warmer lights made the school feel more like a home than an institution, and teachers added to this feeling by placing lamps in their rooms, including ones at their desks.

Judy Thompson, a physical education teacher, started the year teaching in three different schools. She commented that her mood and energy level was notably different at one of the schools even though the schools were similar in many ways. She finally traced the difference to the fact that the hallways and classrooms in the third school were much brighter than at the other two—they felt dark and depressing inside. Would a coat of white paint brighten up your school? It may improve learning.

> "In a huge recent study, researchers individually interviewed 12,000 students, grades 7–12 about their experience in eight 'high risk' areas. . . . The results of this study were striking. . . . The more connected students felt to their families the less involved they were in risky behaviors. The other major factor, and here is the relevance to school safety and school-based character education, was feeling connected to school —feeling close to people at school, feeling fairly treated by teachers, feeling part of one's school."
> —Eric Schaps, author (2000)

Another school exchanged its harsh-sounding bells for gentler sounds; the new tones are much more soothing and far less institutional. (Most "tone" systems can be adjusted in this way.) Together with community members, Asbury Elementary painted a 100-foot mural on an outside wall announcing the qualities that it stands for. Students and neighbors get to enjoy it every day. Cory Elementary School, following its Children Practicing Respect assembly, created a display board in the front lobby of the school that features a "respectful" student each month along with a description of why he or she was chosen. They also planted a wonderful "peace garden" in the front of the school.

Teller Elementary School has pictures of many of its students lining its walls. The school's physical education teacher took pictures of students who embody qualities in the Teller touchstone (known as the Teller Promise) such as caring and responsibility and developed posters of these qualities. She writes the names of students who are "caught" demonstrating those behaviors.

A K–8 school selects, frames, and displays student artwork that becomes part of its permanent art collection. Each spring the school holds an arts festival where two pieces of artwork from each student in the school are put on display. Three outside judges then select two pieces from each grade level. These 18 students are invited to donate their work to the school's art collection. This is followed by an all-school assembly where the 18 students describe the vision behind their piece of artwork. This event has turned the school into a permanent student art gallery, which inspires other students to produce their best work. They know they could visit the school 30 years later with their own kids and find their art still hanging in the school.

"If we take care to honor the roots of a tree, then the trunk and branches will take care of themselves."
—Marianne Williamson, author and lecturer

The ways students carry themselves also help shape a school's physical environment. With all else being equal, a school in which students slouch in their seats or practically nap at their desks looks and feels very differently than one in which they sit with good posture, hold their shoulders square, and look the speaker in the eye. One notices the difference that posture and presence make when visiting certain other cultures. For instance, the powerful posture of the Masai tribesmen of Africa and the elegant gait of Balinese women in Indonesia communicate the dignity and beauty of the human form. They radiate a very different energy than do students in schools where "slumpitis" is the norm.

One school decided—as an entire staff—to introduce the ritual of "head and shoulders" for all its students. Notice how the behavioral cues fit together as a coherent package:

• *Head and shoulders:* Students are expected to sit up in class with an awareness of their head and shoulders. The head and eyes are directed toward the speaker and the shoulders are square so the lungs can easily fill with oxygen. Feet are flat on the floor. The student is fully present to the activity at hand. Head and shoulders also apply when standing.

• *Open hand:* Teachers and even students reminded others about posture by holding palms facing upwards next to the waist and then slowly raising them a few inches. The subtle movement is a gentle reminder to be present in mind and body.

• *Hand raised:* When adults in charge of a group setting want everyone's attention, they simply raise their hand and everyone in the room follows suit until the room becomes quiet and everyone is present in their head and shoulders posture.

- *Walking:* Students and staff with head and shoulder presence walk on the right side of hallways and on the appropriate side of stairwells.

None of these signals would work if teachers independently developed their own cues: the power is in the consistency throughout the school.

A school's physical environment can include the surrounding neighborhood as well, which in some cases can be shaped to reflect the values of the school. Several years ago we visited Trinity College in Hartford, Connecticut. The college was like a walled fortress in the midst of urban blight; people viewed the neighborhood as a liability to the school. Then along came a new president who saw the situation through different eyes. He saw the neighborhood as an opportunity for student learning. The city of Hartford joined the college to build and operate an elementary school adjacent to the college. This created wonderful opportunities for both groups to learn from each other and became a popular service-learning site for the college students.

Is there something in your neighborhood that is waiting to be seen with new eyes? A retirement center? A local market? A vacant lot that could be a community garden?

The physical environment "holds" a school and is perhaps the most obvious expression of your culture. Make sure it holds yours well.

"A school can create a coherent environment, a climate, more potent than any single influence—teachers, class, family, neighborhood—so potent that for at least six hours a day it can override almost everything else in the lives of children."
—Ron Edmonds, author (1986)

"[T]o teach is to create a space in which the community of truth is practiced."
—Parker Palmer, author (1998), p. 90

Gateway 7: Markers, Rituals, and Transitions

About twelve years ago, author Charles Elbot conducted an informal survey inquiring into the most meaningful events in the lives of recent high school graduates. He asked these young people what are the moments, events, or experiences that resonated important learning and meaning. He asked them to reflect on any transforming times, powerful initiations, or discovery of important values that altered the course of their lives. After thinking about this inquiry, most young people agreed on one single, life-altering event—getting their driver's license. When he probed further, seeking other important life markers, he was surprised by the lack of powerful school-based experiences that resonated with these recent graduates. To be sure, some students acknowledged that such special experiences as having the lead role in a school play or winning a state athletic championship meant a great deal to them. However, in the majority of discussions he was struck by the paucity of significant markers.

There have been cultures throughout history that have had a keen sense of the power inherent in celebrations, rituals, and rites of passage. Many Native American tribes, for example, understood the importance of marking the transformation from childhood to adulthood. Only some schools recognize the power of learning associated with change. Change in the life of a student is inevitable but growth is optional. Each school has the opportunity to mark change and support student growth. A marker can evolve into a ritual, a rite of passage, a tradition, and/or a yearly celebration. For example, an important transition may initially be designed as a marker and then evolve into a perennial ritual for teachers, a powerful rite of passage for students, and a tradition or celebration for parents. In many cases, a school begins by "marking" a noteworthy moment in time and, when repeated, this intentional marking can grow organically into a ritual, rite of passage, or tradition.

"Students care deeply about learning when their teachers meet their need for affirmation, contribution, purpose, power and challenge."
—Carol Ann Tomlinson, author (2002), p. 7

Why are markers important? For one, a marker can bring a greater consciousness of learning to an underlying process of development. For example, when children enter kindergarten they are on a many-year journey of growth from identifying primarily with "me" to also identifying with "we." Since this development is of such foundational importance, one school marks this learning by having each year's second grade take an overnight trip to Glenwood Springs, a three-hour bus trip into the mountains. Throughout the second-grade year, students and parents raise funds so all of the 50-some students can participate without paying any fees. These months of preparation set the stage for a powerful initiation into a sense of school as a community. In the course of two days, students and staff accomplish a challenging hike to Hanging Lake, play together in the hot springs, sleep on the floor of a local church, learn history and science, set up meals, eat, clean up, support a friend who is homesick or scared, and laugh together. This newly acquired sense of connectedness, of "we," of community, is powerful, indeed!

"In times of great challenge or dynamic change, such as schools are now experiencing, organizations must develop cultures that are significantly different than those needed in stable times."
—Alan Blankstein, author (2004), p. 7

Markers also serve to awaken students to a sudden change in situation. In general, our culture is not very effective in honoring transitions, coming to terms with endings, loss, and new beginnings. Everyone who has been to high school knows that these years are less forgiving than the preceding K–8 school years. Whereas the past academic grades and behavior issues of the earlier school years are long forgiven and forgotten, ninth grade truly does begin to create a permanent record. How many ninth graders are fully aware of the ramifications of their daily choices until it is too late to avoid suffering the consequences?

One middle school marked this change in accountability by having eighth-grade students individually share something they deeply cared about with the whole school, faculty, and students. These speeches would become the main focus of the middle school assembly every Friday afternoon. Sixth graders sat, listened, and wondered what it was about life that they themselves cared deeply about. The reflection intensified for seventh graders as the students realized their turn to share was no longer in the distant future. Students also understood that the more genuine their sharing, the greater the kudos. Yet the question was always present: Can I summon the courage necessary to speak from my heart?

This same middle school honored all eighth graders with a citation written and delivered by a teacher who captured the essence qualities of each student. The four-hour presentation and dinner at the end of the school year created indelible memories for students, teachers, and parents, preparing students for their transition to high school.

Another elementary school had departing fifth graders lead a knighting ceremony for the incoming leaders of the school, the rising fifth graders. Students created a shield that represented their desired life qualities, then painted symbols on their shields that exemplified friendship, perseverance, integrity, teamwork, and excellence. A knighting ceremony followed. We have met adults who participated in this several-day ceremony more than 30 years ago. They remember it like it was yesterday and still have their shield! For some, it is the only physical object from their K–12 years still in their possession.

In cultures where the adult world does not provide meaningful markers, young people tend to create their own. In many schools, the most powerful ritual, tradition, or marker is that of the oldest students (typically 5th, 8th, and 12th graders) intimidating or harassing the younger students. Some other current youth-created markers include joining a gang, doing drugs, binge drinking, body piercing, dropping out of school, teenage pregnancy, breaking the law, and spending time in jail. Writer Michael Meade (1993) notes, "If the fires that innately burn inside youths are not intentionally and lovingly added to the hearth of community, they will burn down the structures of culture, just to feel the warmth" (p. 19).

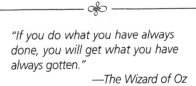

"If you do what you have always done, you will get what you have always gotten."

—The Wizard of Oz

School staffs may want to inquire into three aspects associated with its markers, rituals, traditions, ceremonies, and rites of passage:

1. Which ones are of questionable value?

2. Which ones have deep meaning and are effective for learning and growth?

3. What kinds of new markers are needed to strengthen the school culture?

Some teachers have identified questionable practices such as hazing rituals, the "blame game," endless P.A. announcements, ineffective disciplinary practices, and the loss of important traditions with the arrival of a new principal. Effective practices include opening and closing school-year ceremonies; morning meetings; hallway decorum; teachers greeting every student upon entering their classroom; grade-level, service-learning projects; back-to-school night; beginning-of-the-school-year home visits; cross-grade reading buddies; birthday celebrations; grade-level music programs; and an annual arts festival.

Some commonly missing practices include:

- Welcoming new teachers and families into the school community
- Holding transition rituals for students and staff leaving school
- Initiating commonly practiced school procedures
- Marking the death of a school community member appropriately
- Initiating volunteers into the school culture
- Beginning and ending the school day in a meaningful way
- Developing a ritual for sharing success stories
- Building traditions to support new teachers, such as having every teacher give each new teacher a voucher to take over his or her class for a 30-minute period during their first year of teaching

School life is rich with transitions—both big and small. Yet the full importance of transitions is not well understood. How we join and take leave of a school community can significantly impact us and others. Recently we worked with a school that was undergoing intense trauma. Their new principal had not worked out. The former principal, who had been highly regarded, had left suddenly in August for another school district after seven years as principal at the school. The faculty did not have the chance to adjust to this sudden loss or to transition to the new leadership. At the first faculty meeting in August, the newly appointed principal stepped on two cultural "land mines" from which he never recovered. When a teacher asked about having her own child at school on an inservice day, the principal said "no." When another teacher inquired if a colleague could watch her students if she needed to leave early for a doctor's appointment, the principal responded, "You should take a personal day," not realizing that most of these teachers saved these precious personal days for when their own children were sick.

In a brief two minutes, the majority of the school's faculty and staff experienced the loss of two precious privileges they had enjoyed over the past seven years. The principal had no idea what had just happened and had no clue as to the explosions that were reverberating inside the heads of everyone in the room. These two missteps, which occurred before there was a chance to build relationships and trust, doomed this principal from the first day. He had no idea what was "sacred" in this school culture. As a result, many teachers did not volunteer for committees or extra duties and sometimes were reluctant to "go the extra mile" for a student.

Clearly, the principal was going by the book and was not aware of the underlying "give-and-take" culture that had evolved at the school. In this particular situation, everyone—students, teachers, and principal—lost out. Had the principal's awareness of entering a new culture been more finely tuned, he might have responded to these inquiries by saying, "We will follow past practices until I come to understand more about how things work here. You have a very successful school here. Let me learn about you before we change anything." It is not unusual for a new principal to change long-standing practices and traditions without the awareness of their meaning and effectiveness. How things are done at a school needs to be approached with respect and insight!

In a similar manner, many schools do not guide departures from its community. A student may fail to show up for school one day, never to return again. Days later the school receives a notice from another school to forward the student's records. Since the loss of his teachers, friends, and school was not consciously acknowledged, the student may well enter his new school community with anxiety instead of an adventurous attitude.

"We, as educators, must find that balance between the world of the mind and that of the heart and soul. It is the mind that preoccupies our time and that will take us to the information age. But it is the heart and soul that will allow us to remain connected to our humanity that will build that bridge between us . . . and create a good society."
—Paul Houston, author (1998), p. 53

A thoughtful school culture should have structured processes for properly joining and leaving a school community for all its members—students, parents, and staff. We suggest one such structure as introducing the new community member to the school's touchstone. Parents could be given a magnet with the touchstone, and the new staff member or student could be invited to sign the school's touchstone banner. When a student leaves a school for another, there could be a specific departure ritual in the classroom and a good wishes handshake with the principal. This kind of leaving can bring confidence instead of anxiety to the person who is separating from one school and about to enter a new one. It can also bring closure to those left behind.

It takes time, awareness, and the question "How are things done here?" to read a new culture. Once you have some understanding of a new culture, you can participate in changing it. But a culture can only change from where it is at in a given moment of time. Without this fundamental respect, the act of trying to change it could be an act of aggression. Too often we enter into a new situation with our enthusiasm to bring all the great things that have worked from our past, but we are oblivious to what is going on right in front of us. We fail to see the new situation in all of its freshness. Our sight is clouded by comparing it with our past experiences and our desires for the future. We have witnessed students, staff, and parents offend others in their first days of entering into a new culture. How many times have we heard a new teacher, principal, or student say, "We did it this way at my old school," meaning my old school did it better but not realizing that what we are promoting is usually what is most familiar to ourselves—not necessarily better or worse—just different.

Schools have a tremendous potential to shape "how" things are done every moment of the school day. Markers, rituals, and thoughtful transitions can serve as effective tools to develop more conscious ways of being.

Gateway 8: Leadership

Edgar Shein (1992) wrote in *Organizational Culture and Leadership* that "the only thing of real importance that leaders do is create and manage culture" (p. 11). This gateway explores leadership in terms of the four tools that create and manage school culture.

The first tool, a schoolwide touchstone, can only become a vibrant part of daily school life through leadership. Skillful leaders can take a school community through the process of identifying values that the community should hold on to, values that it needs to let go of, and those new values that it needs to embrace. Leaders can provide the environment for community members to gain understanding and ownership of each of these guiding principles and integrate them into the life of the school. However, over time a touchstone can become stale and a creative leader can find ways to keep it vital. At several schools, for instance, the principal and teachers used drama to infuse new life into the touchstone.

"Effective leaders know that the hard work of reculturing is the sine qua non of progress."
—Michael Fullan, author
(2001), p. 44

An example of community leadership can be found at Carson Elementary. The school gathered 23 participants consisting of teachers, paraprofessionals, parents, and the principal "to gain a greater understanding of how we can work to create an intentional school culture as it relates to our touchstone," as the invitation to the event announced. Through a series of meetings throughout a school year the school not only made improvements but also discovered an effective leadership forum. The principal stated

> The communication between members of the Planning Committee proved to be so productive that part of the action plan of this group is to meet periodically to continue open dialogue and to seek opportunities for collaboration on future projects. Rather than a single theme, the Planning Committee seems to be evolving into an

ongoing process of shared reflection and communication to promote growth in our students and our community.

At South High School, a single teacher initiated a student movement to create a "campaign of influence" around positive character traits. They created a creed that was hung on banners in the school and on a moveable standard that was placed at school activities, including sporting events, school plays and concerts, and assemblies. Their campaign of influence has led to service-learning activities, "the best assembly seen at South" (according to the teacher) and plans to bring peer mediation and Peace Jam to South High School. Leadership does not stop with teachers. Student leadership, parent leadership, and community leadership are all associated with effective schools.

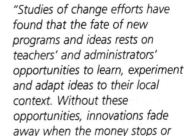

"Studies of change efforts have found that the fate of new programs and ideas rests on teachers' and administrators' opportunities to learn, experiment and adapt ideas to their local context. Without these opportunities, innovations fade away when the money stops or the enforcement pressures end."
—Linda Darling-Hammond, Stanford University professor

We have already explored the relationship between leadership and the Four Mind-Set Model. However, it is important to remember that without leadership it is highly unlikely that students, staff, and parents will readily think and act out of more highly integrated mind-sets. Most of us resist change; yet appropriate leadership can be the catalyst to move us through the disequilibrium that most change requires. Moreover, the dominant mind-set of the principal has a disproportionate impact on the larger school culture. The style of a very hierarchical and dependent-minded principal can overpower even the most collaborative staff.

Leadership is extremely important in working with the eight gateways. Which gateway should a school enter first, the one that is least understood and most problematic or the one that is most accessible and will build experience and confidence? There are no easy answers. A combination of the collective wisdom of the group and keen leadership can often make the best choice.

"Structural change that is not supported by cultural change will eventually be overwhelmed by the culture, for it is in the culture that any organization finds meaning and stability."
—Phillip Schlechty, author (1997)

Here we explore the fourth tool of learning and adapting from other cultures at greater length. Too often educators see their field as so unique that they have little to gain from looking at other cultures, and this self-imposed isolation has not served education well. A strong leader can help a staff and school community pull back the blinders and explore what else is out there.

Every culture has its strengths and weaknesses. A particular practice or quality in one culture might be highly refined and enlightening; yet this same culture may also have some characteristics that are limiting. Cultures can learn and adapt from each other while retaining their basic integrity. As Montaigne wrote 400 years ago:

> The bees plunder the flowers here and there, but afterward they make of them honey, which is all theirs; it is no longer thyme or marjoram. Even so, with the pieces borrowed from others, he will transform and blend them to make a work that is all his own.

Creating your own unique school culture, while borrowing from the work of others, is such a task.

Here are a few examples of "bees plundering the flowers here and there." We can learn much from professions outside of education. We have given some examples of learning from the business culture and will now show some ways that we can learn from the medical world. For instance, the U.S. medical profession is now training doctors to empathize with patients in order to deliver care more effectively. Realizing that the present structure of training doctors contributes to "ethical erosion"—becoming desensitized to the physical suffering and minor indignities of being a patient—Harvard is piloting a program to make training more patient centered. Third-year students are now paired with a chronically ill patient for five months and accompany him or her to every visit with a health care provider. (Being a relatively healthy group, few medical students have ever experienced chronic illness themselves.) This has led to new under-standings of being a patient and to better care. One student, for example, gained important insights into why a diabetic patient did not take her insulin and was therefore able to correct the problem and improve her health. Nathan Thornburgh wrote in *Time* magazine that doctors who try to understand their patients may be the best antidote for the widespread dissatisfaction with today's healthcare system" (p. 58).

Are there structures in schooling that contribute to the "ethical erosion" of our teachers and limit empathy for students? Have many of us forgotten what it is like to be a student—to be shuttled from classroom to classroom every 45 minutes, to sit at a desk in hot classrooms for six hours a day, and to attend classes in which you may feel incompetent? Perhaps more teachers should spend a day as a student to be reminded of what it is like.

Just as medical students and doctors tend to be healthier than their patients perhaps we teachers have forgotten what it is like to struggle aca-demically in a particular subject. Of course adding polynomials is easy if you have been teaching algebra for ten years, but what if it is your first time and math has never been a strong subject for you? Perhaps we teachers should be required to learn something new on a regular basis—a musical instrument, a foreign language, a difficult skill at home repair—just to be reminded of how difficult and at times humiliating (but also exhilarating) learning something new can be.

According to Dr. Erik Alexander of Brigham and Women's Hospital in Boston, the old model and old culture of training doctors prevented them from seeing the patient as a whole person; patients were shuttled throughout the system to treat their various symptoms. This led to a splintering of care and a mind-set in which doctors viewed patients narrowly. The best doctors in the future, he says, will bring a different mind-set and treat the patient as a whole individual, not merely as a series of symptoms. But as he suggests, this will require shifting the culture of hospitals and of medical schools.

How do we create a culture in our schools that encourages and rewards us for viewing students as whole human beings? Are there presently structures and norms that encourage just the opposite—a splintering of care—in our own profession?

A recent study regarding another aspect of the medical profession is relevant to the field of education. The study found that the organizational culture of some hospitals discourages nurses and other employees from reporting medical errors or other lapses in patient care, which delays fixing these problems. The authors concluded that this was a result of norms that promote individualism and self-sufficiency instead of a collaborative commitment to patient care (Tucker & Edmondson, 2003). This is also true at many schools where teachers and other staff members are reluctant to report poor practice or other "system failures," even though doing so might improve learning. Perhaps similar cultural norms are at play: a belief that it is "none of my business" what goes on in the classroom next door, even if that teacher shows videos each day and the students learn little. Are schools learning all they can from where they fall short? How can we transform a school culture from rewarding self-sufficiency and individualism to rewarding learning and improvement, collaboration, and understanding the interconnectedness of school goals?

The current school reform movement is based largely on transforming the teacher-centered, individualistic approach of educating young people to one of teaching to specific statewide academic standards and being held accountable through state assessments. As education is reaping gains from this change, few educators are asking what else they are getting along with these reforms. It is important to explore how this shift may be impacting teachers, students, and their families. The medical profession provides a cautionary tale of what happens when a profession does not tend to the hearts of its practitioners.

"Change in teaching for more effective learning requires major transformation in the culture of the school. . . ."
—Michael Fullan, author

It was not too many decades ago that the medical profession operated on the strengths of a doctor's intuition and bedside manner. As scientific knowledge increased, the practice of medicine shifted to one of expertise, which has greatly enhanced medical effectiveness. The medical profession, however, has at the same time shed itself of some of its humanity. Healing came to be understood as a set of clinical procedures done to parts of a patient's body through a set of impersonalized acts. A nephrologist might see someone as a kidney, just as a math teacher might see their students only as test scores. How has this shift in the medical profession affected its practitioners and what if anything can the K–12 teaching profession learn from this experience as it moves toward greater objectivity and expertise?

Dr. Rachel Naomi Remen (1999) wrote in *The Heart of Learning*, "It took me many years to realize that medical education is not an education at all: it is a training. An education evokes wholeness and attends to integrity, while a training specializes, focuses, and narrows us" (p. 36). The kinds of concerns expressed by Dr. Remen about the medical profession are beginning to be heard in public schooling. We propose that the "disconnect" that has evolved in medical practice is very similar to what is happening to the teachers of our K–12 schools and is reflected in their low sense of well-being. Our challenge in education is to continue to develop our knowledge and expertise as associated with the sciences of teaching and learning while attending to our own wholeness, the wholeness of colleagues, and the wholeness of our students.

"If the educators don't take the lead in shaping their school's culture, then other forces will shape it for them."

—Charles Elbot, author

The medical profession is developing ways to heal the wounds of its culture. Perhaps educators can learn from their strategies before too much damage is done.

Teachers experience loss and disappointment on a daily basis, from losing students of high mobility to having students fall short of expectations. As teachers move from being educators to trainers, they are losing touch with their own sense of wholeness. Teachers might feel that the curriculum is not one of their choosing, that the parent community fluctuates as parents shop for schools or move around in our transient society, that colleagues with whom they are compared and with whom they compete no longer provide safe harbors; that school leaders are under so much pressure to succeed that they can no longer confide in them; that professional growth no longer includes personal growth; that the profession they entered into to serve the hearts and minds of young people is being reduced to training for knowledge and skills as mandated by state accountability assessments.

"Changing a toxic school culture into a healthy school culture that inspires lifelong learning among students and adults is the greatest challenge of instructional leadership."

—Roland S. Barth, author (2002)

How can educational leaders and the teaching profession align expertise and wholeness? How can they align the head and the heart? We need to make progress in both domains and learn from other cultures that have traveled this road. Effective leadership can make sure these conversations are on the table.

Leadership is a critical factor in creating and managing a school culture. Doug Reeves, the founder of the Center for Performance Assessment, wrote in the December 2006/ January 2007 issue of *Educational Leadership*: "Meaningful school improvement begins with cultural change—and cultural change begins with the school leader" (p. 92).

It is through leadership that we will attend to the wholeness of teachers and their students. It is leadership that will give rise to an effective schoolwide touchstone that elevates our thoughts and actions. It is leadership that introduces and effectively employs the Four Mind-Set Model and accesses the eight gateways. It is through leadership that a school can take advantage of wisdom from other cultures to intentionally build excellence in all the school aspires toward. In a commentary in *Education Week,* Patrick Bassett (2005) applies lessons from a *The Harvard Business Review* article, "The Seven Surprises for New CEOs," to new school leaders. He states that the responsibilities of school leaders involve "maintaining a salubrious climate and building a culture that supports teachers and makes it possible for children to learn. If the new school leader gets that right, most else will follow in due course" (p. 36).

> "The Toyota Way involves the company learning from its mistakes, determining the root cause of problems, providing effective countermeasures, empowering people to implement those measures, and having a process for transferring the new knowledge to the right people to make it part of the company's repertoire of understanding and behavior."
>
> —Jeffrey Liker, author (2004), p. 251

RESOURCE T: EIGHT GATEWAYS ASSESSMENT TOOL

Gateway 1: Teaching, Learning, and Assessment

The norms of good teaching and learning constitute an important aspect of school culture. At the best schools, these norms are transparent and widely shared.

Beliefs and practices about how to assess student learning also become embedded in a school culture. Assessments can help *enhance* learning—by providing regular and useful feedback, by providing multiple opportunities to demonstrate mastery, and so on—or simply to *verify* learning. The best schools keep a balance.

Reflections

Rate how your school relates to teaching and assessment, based on the following criteria. Add up your score at the bottom.

1 = Strongly disagree
2 = Disagree
3 = Neutral
4 = Agree
5 = Strongly agree

_____ 1. There is wide agreement among teachers in my school about what constitutes high-quality teaching and learning.

_____ 2. A large percentage of teachers in my school engage in high-quality teaching.

_____ 3. Groups of teachers meet regularly to look at student work to improve teaching, learning, and assessment.

_____ 4. There are structures in place (e.g., visiting each other's classroom, critical friends' circles) for teachers to receive feedback from each other on their teaching.

_____ 5. Assessments (tests, quizzes, projects, portfolios, presentations, etc.) are used in a balanced way to both enhance and verify learning.

_____ TOTAL SCORE

Gateway 2: Relationships

The quality of relationships between students, staff, and parents plays a prominent part in any school's culture. Students who feel cared about and connect to their teachers are significantly more likely to engage in the learning process. Yale child psychiatrist James Comer (2004), a student of school improvement, aptly notes that significant learning requires a significant relationship.

The quality of relationships between the adults in the building (teachers and staff) and parents also is important. Care, trust, and support among the adults constitute a significant resource for creating and honoring shared agreements that promote student learning. On the other hand, students can almost immediately detect when staff are not on the same page on significant issues.

Reflections

Rate how your school relates to the quality of relationships based on the following criteria. Add up your score at the bottom.

1 = Strongly disagree
2 = Disagree
3 = Neutral
4 = Agree
5 = Strongly agree

_____ 1. The school effectively uses information collected formally and informally from students about how cared for and connected to teachers they feel.

_____ 2. The tone of voice between students and staff is respectful, appropriate, and at times even lighthearted. There is little or no yelling at students in the halls or classrooms.

_____ 3. Staff care for and support each other both professionally and personally. Humor and laughter are evident in staff meetings, classrooms, and halls.

_____ 4. The staff and administration generally enjoy a healthy and productive relationship.

_____ 5. Parents generally enjoy a healthy and productive relationship with the school.

_____ TOTAL SCORE

Gateway 3: Problem Solving

How an organization faces challenges and solves its problems says a lot about its culture. At some organizations, upper management "solves" all the problems, whereas collaboration is the norm elsewhere. Some organizations, such as Toyota, encourage their employees to point out mistakes (so they can be fixed), whereas other organizations effectively punish employees for doing so.

(Continued)

RESOURCE T   (Continued)

Reflections

Rate how your school relates to problem solving based on the following criteria. Add up your score at the bottom.

1 = Strongly disagree
2 = Disagree
3 = Neutral
4 = Agree
5 = Strongly agree

_____ 1. My school approaches issues proactively instead of reactively.

_____ 2. My school works to get at the root of problems instead of just treating symptoms.

_____ 3. My school approaches problems and issues collaboratively (when appropriate) instead of having the principal try to solve everything.

_____ 4. My school works effectively with parents and home to resolve student issues that require this partnership.

_____ 5. My school skillfully distinguishes between those problems that call for staff input (and perhaps consensus) and those that can be handled by the person in charge.

_____ TOTAL SCORE

Gateway 4: Expectations, Trust, and Accountability

Expectations are like magnets: they can either stretch people to the top end of their performance range or pull them down. High expectations can even expand one's performance range by fostering growth. This is most likely to occur in a school when an entire staff—not just a few teachers—reinforce high expectations.

Both academic and character expectations matter. Not only do we want to challenge students to use their minds well, we want to challenge them to be their most respectful, responsible, and caring selves. Schools can help by paying attention to the ethical climate of the school. For instance, policies and practices that discourage cheating are helpful, as are efforts to promote civility in school. Also, opportunities for ethical action, such as through service learning and schoolwide service rituals, communicate important expectations.

Reflections

Rate how your school relates to expectations based on the following criteria. Add up your score at the bottom.

1 = Strongly disagree
2 = Disagree
3 = Neutral
4 = Agree
5 = Strongly agree

_____ 1. The vast majority of teachers in my school hold high academic expectations, and this is evident through their rigorous instruction.

_____ 2. The vast majority of teachers in my school hold high character expectations (e.g., they discourage cheating and insist on respectful behavior).

_____ 3. My school effectively communicates high expectations to parents.

_____ 4. Mechanisms are in place to provide timely and effective feedback to teachers or staff members who are not "carrying their load" (e.g., not expecting much of kids academically, not fulfilling playground duty).

_____ 5. Teachers strive to stretch each child, regardless of his or her present level of performance, and recognize that some students will take longer to learn certain concepts.

_____ TOTAL SCORE

Gateway 5: Voice

Voice reflects how much one feels "heard" at school. Students who report feeling heard by teachers and administration feel more connected to their school and more invested in their own learning. Unfortunately, many students report feeling like passengers in their school.

Schools that nurture an appropriate expression of student voice create structures for this end and these include an active student council and a strategy for regularly soliciting student feedback. They also employ teaching strategies, such as service learning, that develop voice.

Both teacher voice and parent voice are also important. As with students, when teachers and parents feel heard, they feel more ownership in the success of the school.

Reflections

Rate how your school relates to voice based on the following criteria. Add up your scores at the bottom.

1 = Strongly disagree
2 = Disagree
3 = Neutral

RESOURCE T   (Continued)

4 = Agree
5 = Strongly agree

_____ 1. The school has effective structures and processes such as student council and other student groups that provide opportunities for students to be heard by teachers and administration.

_____ 2. The school regularly solicits feedback from students about what is working and what can be improved at school and in specific classrooms. Students—especially at the elementary level—have an opportunity to shape classroom norms, and so forth.

_____ 3. There is a schoolwide commitment to using teaching strategies that develop student voice. These might include service learning, book fairs, Socratic teaching, and providing appropriate choice about books and projects.

_____ 4. Teachers and staff are invited, when appropriate, to provide input on important school decisions. Generally there is healthy and productive communication between staff and administration.

_____ 5. Parents express an appropriate degree of voice at school, including serving on committees.

_____ TOTAL SCORE

Gateway 6: Physical Environment

A school's physical environment, both inside and outside, is a resource that can be shaped to enhance learning. The physical space "holds" members of a school community and can foster a sense of well-being in them. An environment that fails to hold and nurture people can negatively impact many aspects of a school.

Reflections

Rate how your school relates to physical space based on the following criteria. Add up your score at the bottom.

1 = Strongly disagree
2 = Disagree
3 = Neutral
4 = Agree
5 = Strongly agree

_____ 1. My school is safe, orderly, and welcoming.

_____ 2. My school's physical environment, including classrooms, hallways, and library, is deliberately shaped by teachers and students to inspire learning.

_____ 3. My school takes advantage of its surrounding physical environment, such as the neighborhood, a larger city, and state. (For example, our fourth graders do a year-long study of the ecology of a pond in the park across from our school.)

_____ 4. My school prominently displays student work in classrooms and hallways.

_____ 5. My school deliberately creates unique physical spaces (a welcoming entranceway with coffee, a parent workroom, a peace garden, a welcoming faculty room, etc.) that communicate who we are.

_____ TOTAL SCORE

Gateway 7: Markers, Rituals, and Transitions

Markers highlight important moments for an individual, group, or larger community. For instance, a school might choose to mark the transition from fifth grade to sixth grade or to celebrate the career of a teacher who is retiring. If repeated, a marker can develop into a ritual or regular rite of passage, as in the case of new sixth graders. It is these markers, in their many forms, that give meaning, depth, and connectedness to important aspects of a school's culture and to the people in it.

Reflections

Rate how your school relates to markers, rituals, and rites of passage on the following criteria. Add up your score at the bottom.

1 = Strongly disagree
2 = Disagree
3 = Neutral
4 = Agree
5 = Strongly agree

_____ 1. We have meaningful markers, rituals, rites of passage, traditions, and celebrations at my school.

_____ 2. My school is free from questionable traditions and norms such as student hazing and destructive staff gossip.

_____ 3. My school allows outdated rituals and traditions to gracefully die and is open to forming new ones as needed.

_____ 4. My school has initiation rituals that introduce new staff and families to the school's values and traditions.

_____ 5. My school has ceremonies that honor and support its vision, such as an annual student arts festival and a parent appreciation breakfast.

_____ TOTAL SCORE

(Continued)

RESOURCE T   (Continued)

Gateway 8: Leadership

Edgar Shein (1992) wrote in *Organizational Culture and Leadership* that "the only thing of real importance that leaders do is create and manage culture" (p. 11). Leaders who do this well empower those around them to find ways to support the mission, vision, and values of the school. In a school with a strong culture of leadership, the administration, teachers, students, and parents are all empowered to lead. In such a school, you would find teacher-leaders attending math conferences and sharing new knowledge with colleagues, you would find student-leaders organizing other students to improve the school, and you would find a principal skillfully creating and managing projects and processes to keep the school running smoothly.

Reflections

Rate how your school relates to leadership based on the following criteria. Add up your score at the bottom.

1 = Strongly disagree
2 = Disagree
3 = Neutral
4 = Agree
5 = Strongly agree

_____ 1. Leaders make it clear that their most important work is to create and manage a school culture, including aligning the culture of the individual classroom with the larger school culture.

_____ 2. Leaders keep current on the latest theory and research on schooling and leadership to create an effective school.

_____ 3. We maximize the strengths of our school (e.g., the neighborhood, the student diversity) and minimize its weaknesses (e.g., crowded conditions) to enhance student learning.

_____ 4. As leaders, we learn and appropriately adapt best practices from other cultures to improve our school.

_____ 5. As a school, we actively develop leadership qualities such as listening, consensus-building, and empowerment in staff, students, and parents.

_____ TOTAL SCORE

RESOURCE U: SCORING SHEET

Directions:

Transfer the total score for each of the eight gateways next to the labels below. Based on the scores, consider which gateway to develop first. Consider taking this instrument again in a few months to chart progress.

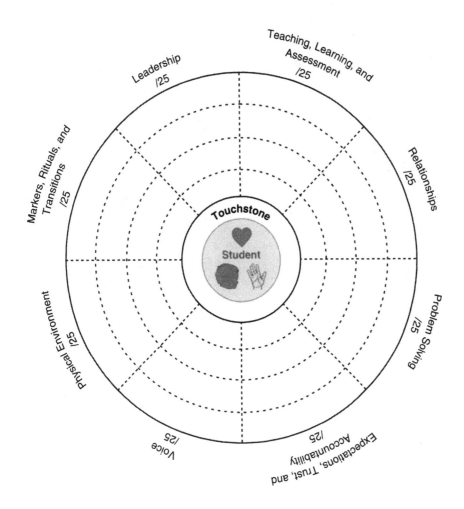

RESOURCE V: STAFF REFLECTION TOOL

Thank you for participating in a pilot of the staff reflection tool at Montview. This tool provides valuable feedback and will validate strengths and identify opportunities for growth. Please circle an E (Exceeds), M (Meets), or N (Does Not Meet) for how well you feel that each staff member upholds the shared agreements below. Leave a category blank if you feel you lack enough information to provide meaningful feedback. Also, feel free to include comments.

This staff reflection is entirely anonymous. Each staff member will receive his or her own results, which will not be seen by any other staff member, including the administration. This is not an evaluation; it is for your own benefit and that of the whole school. We encourage you to meet with a trusted colleague to review your feedback, which you should receive next week.

	Exceeds Montview Expectations	Meets Montview Expectations	Does Not Meet Montview Expectations
Relations with and expectations of students	Almost always speaks to students in a respectful tone Is seen as an advocate for children Finds a way to stretch all students academically Has exceptional rapport with students	Usually speaks to students in a respectful tone, even when disciplining them; rarely yells Challenges students academically and is seen as a strong teacher Has positive rapport with students	Often speaks to students in a negative tone and even yells at them Regularly complains about students in teachers lounge, etc. Does not challenge students academically

	Exceeds Montview Expectations	Meets Montview Expectations	Does Not Meet Montview Expectations
Team Player	Initiates opportunities to work and plan with others Attends team meetings regularly and contributes positively Others seek out to work with Verbally and actively supports peers, the school, and the district	Works cooperatively with others when part of a team Attends team meetings and participates in team activities Named by others as a person they like to work with Generally supportive of peers, the school, and the district	Singularly focused on his or her own classroom Exhibits negative or apathetic behavior Frequently misses or comes late to meetings Not perceived by others as a team player Bad-mouths the school or district

Staff	Relations and Expectations			Team Player			Comments (optional)
Ben C.	E	M	N	E	M	N	
Charles V.	E	M	N	E	M	N	
Brian B.	E	M	N	E	M	N	
Charlotte V.	E	M	N	E	M	N	

THE INTENTIONAL SCHOOL CULTURE

The Application of the Four Tools

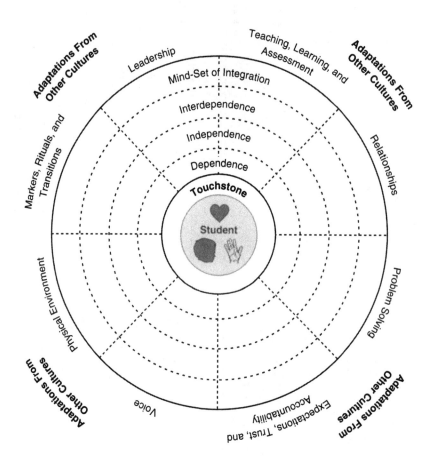

5

Applying the Four Tools

We have made the case for intentionally building a school culture and presented four tools to help you do so: the touchstone, the Four Mind-Set Model, the eight gateways, and the tool of adapting practices from other industries and cultures. We now summarize the main points and put the tools together.

The touchstone is a tool for "how" things are done at a school; it does not focus on the purpose of a school's existence (mission) or where a school is going (vision). Three schools can have similar missions and visions but value very different processes for achieving them. One school might be highly goal oriented and autocratic while another school could be very accommodating and endlessly collaborative. A third school might have a culture based on courageous conversations and authenticity.

In the first school, the ends might typically justify the means; in the second school, the process seems to overshadow everything else perhaps even to the detriment of achieving its goals; and in the third school, thriving requires skillful communication. The school's touchstone informs and guides members of a school community how to go about their lives of teaching and learning.

The Four Mind-Set Model helps to identify the dominant mind-sets of your school and invites more highly integrated ways of thinking and acting. For instance when a faculty discovers the degree to which their

"*The real voyage of discovery consists, not of seeking new landscapes, but in seeing through new eyes.*"
—Marcel Proust,
French novelist and essayist

actions are entrenched in the paradigm of independence, they can become motivated to explore other paradigms such as interdependence. That does not mean being primarily "independent" is wrong, it is just limiting. The same is true of any single paradigm. Synergy is created when schools use the best from all three paradigms: This is the wisdom of integration.

Since school culture covers enormous area, the eight gateways provide a tool for gaining access to the whole through its parts. It is not advisable or even possible to work with every aspect of a school's culture at the same time. The gateways offer ways of thinking about and working effectively with specific aspects of one's culture. As mentioned earlier, it is best to use the gateways after the "big rocks" of a school's culture have been identified (possibly through the School Culture Survey) and addressed.

The tool of adapting insights and constructs from other cultures acknowledges that as educators we do not have all of the answers; this tool taps into the existing and the emerging wisdom of other professions, businesses, and ethnic cultures.

> "Problems cannot be solved at the same level of awareness that created them."
> —Albert Einstein, German physicist and Nobel Prize winner

Each of these four tools on its own has the integrity to make a difference in developing a school's culture. When used in concert, however, these tools can powerfully shape school culture to enhance student learning. Below is a timeline and a road map for using these tools over a two-year period. We realize however that because of other initiatives, some schools are unable to follow each step of the process. Therefore in the next section, we address how a school with more limited time might approach using these tools. We also address some of the challenges that schools might face during the overall process of shaping their culture.

Timeline: The First 36 Weeks

Year 1 of the initial two school years of building an intentional school

1. Read and discuss the book *Building an Intentional School Culture: Excellence in Academics and Character* (Elbot & Fulton, 2008). (4 weeks)
    - Have discussion groups to understand the nature of this work and to analyze particular aspects that are especially pertinent to your school.
    - Consider staff visits to schools with healthy cultures.
    - Form a school culture committee.

2. Develop a schedule for implementation based on the suggested time line and the needs of your school. Identify all of the great things you are already doing (e.g., service learning) and ensure that they continue. (2 weeks)

3. Take a deep look at your school culture. (6 weeks)
   - Analyze past school surveys for insights into your school culture.
   - Use a school culture survey to gain input from students, parents, and staff, and consider conducting interviews or focus groups with these stakeholders.
   - Ask students, staff, and parents to respond on posters to the following questions: "What do I want to preserve?" and "What do I want to change?" at this school.
   - Compile and synthesize the data. Identify patterns, mind-sets, and weakest links.

4. Build your school's touchstone using the insights from your review of your school culture. (6 weeks)
   - Use the distillation process (see Resource B at end of Chapter 2) to identify the important values of your school and to ensure that they are identified in a democratic manner.
   - Circulate a draft of your touchstone to all school constituents for feedback.
   - Craft and finalize your touchstone.
   - Print the touchstone on student ID cards, classroom posters, magnets for parents, and in your newsletter; read it as part of morning announcements.
   - Follow the enclosed suggestions for a touchstone banner signing ceremony.
   - Analyze how programs (e.g., afterschool programs) and aspects of the school relate to the touchstone; consider strengthening those that support the values in the touchstone and altering or eliminating those that don't.
   - Commit to making the touchstone values be the guiding principles for life at your school.

5. Conduct an inservice on the proper use of your touchstone and begin to build rubrics for each of the values. (6 weeks)
   - Use the touchstone rubrics with students to gain self-awareness and depth of understanding of each virtue.
   - Consider holding regular school assemblies to deepen awareness of using the touchstone.
   - Connect the touchstone qualities with the curriculum (e.g., how the virtue of "courage" is reflected in the literature in English class or in events discussed in history class).

6. Build shared agreements among staff (e.g., being a team player, engaging students intellectually) and link them to the touchstone. (4 weeks)
   - Build rubrics for these agreements.
   - Set two peer reflection times per year for staff to provide feedback to one another.

7. Continue to find ways to further integrate the touchstone into your school culture. (7 weeks)

8. Review the past 35 weeks of implementation. (1 week)

Timeline: The Second 36 Weeks

Year 2 of the initial two school years of building an intentional school

1. Introduce the school's touchstone to new staff, students, and parents. (2 weeks)

2. Use the touchstone throughout the school while exploring the Four Mind-Set Models and how they apply to staff, students, and parents. (8 weeks)
   • Use the faculty and staff Four Mind-Set Model to think and work in more highly integrated ways.
   • Use the Student Four Mind-Set Model to enhance student engagement.
   • Use the Parent Four Mind-Set Model to partner with parents in more highly integrated ways.

3. Introduce the eight gateways and the notion of adapting insights and new approaches from other cultures. (4 weeks)
   • Have the faculty respond to the 40 questions on the Eight Gateways Assessment Tool.
   • Use the results to identify the relative strengths and weaknesses of these eight aspects of your school culture.
   • Find consensus on which gateway to focus on first, and create a plan of action.
   • Review what other schools and organizations have developed in this area, and see what is adaptable to your school culture.

4. Implement your plan for this gateway. (22 weeks)

5. When you have gained a good footing after working with one or two gateways, begin working with the other gateways while still using the school touchstone and referencing the Four Mind-Set Models.
   • Periodically review the touchstone for possible changes. Take the Touchstone Effectiveness Assessment to gauge how well-integrated the touchstone is within your culture.
   • Continue to draw insights from other schools, organizations, and professions.

6. Continue to build your intentional school culture using all four tools and any other means that prove effective.

Although we give examples of how schools can draw from the wisdom of other cultures, we leave it to you to explore this question more fully.

Creative and thoughtful people in other schools, industries, or even countries are constantly exploring new ways to address issues that are likely relevant to your school. It would be unfortunate if we did not draw from their experiences and instead kept doing things the same old way, assuming that the issues facing us are unique.

Pulling It All Together

How do these tools fit together and how might they be used in a school? What should school faculty and staff do if they don't have time to implement all the steps in the process (or all of the tools) outlined in the book? Also, what are some of the challenges that schools typically face when shaping their culture, and how can we address these challenges? We address these questions in the following sections.

First, what are some of the challenges facing schools during a process of shaping their culture? The process is rarely smooth or linear and may take place in fits and starts. Below are responses to questions we have been asked about this process.

- *What if the staff is negative and doesn't seem interested in change?*

We have found that appealing to the staff's own enlightened self-interest is helpful. What's in it for them? Usually when we meet with a staff we ask them: What difference would it make if the quality of the school culture was improved by 10 percent? How would it affect them personally and professionally? How would it affect students?

Through discussion and sharing-out, enough positive energy usually emerges to motivate a shifting culture. Imagining even a slightly better state of affairs can prove motivating. Often the schools hurting the most climb on board most easily, while schools where everything seems fine can be harder to motivate. In those cases, data sometimes can prove helpful. We worked with one middle school where the teachers and staff all got along well, and relations with students were also positive. However the school received a "low" rating from the state. Reminding the school about this point and asking what it would take to be rated "average" provided the necessary motivation for change. The school found that it lacked an "edge": Things had become a bit too comfortable there.

We have also found that an ostensibly negative staff can reflect the loud voices of only a few very negative staff members; they can sway staff members who are otherwise more positive. In this regard, the School Culture Survey or the Rubric of Faculty Interdependence can be very helpful. When staff members analyze the data and discover, for instance, that 80 percent of the staff report they like to work at the school or believe that the school is "heading in the right direction," then the power of those few very negative voices become neutralized.

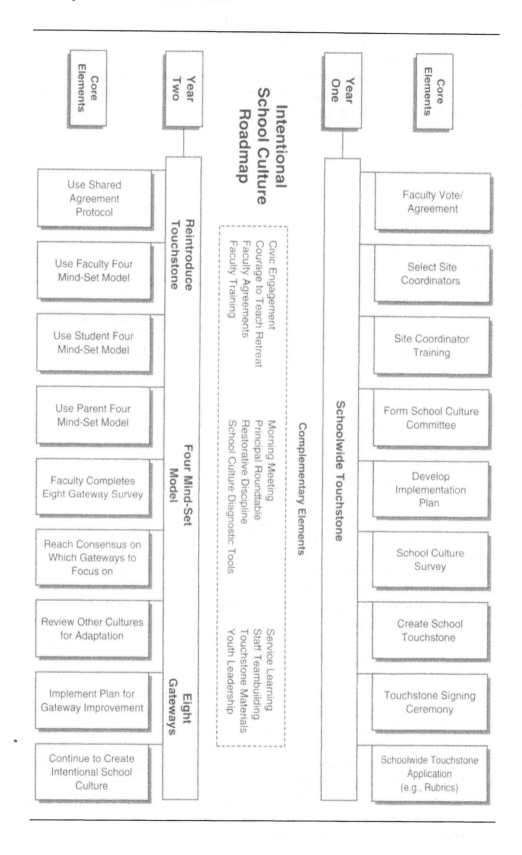

- *What if you don't have time to implement the whole process outlined in this book—where should I start?*

Some schools have such a full plate that fully implementing the process laid out in this book can seem daunting. Here are a few things to keep in mind. First, we have found that the schools that take the long view of building a school culture end up being the most successful. The adage "slow and steady wins the race" seems apt here. For example, Carson Elementary School has put energy into building and maintaining an effective school culture committee composed of staff and parents. They meet monthly and have slowly but intentionally tended to the culture of the school. They take the time to do things right. Their work is neither flashy nor in response to immediate crises; rather the committee has identified and addressed the "big rocks" facing their school. For instance, they have made great strides in helping to mix students socially from three distinct programs within the school. Schools without a functional culture committee will likely tend to their culture only episodically or during times of crisis. We feel this is the wrong way to go about it.

Second, if a school doesn't have time for the whole process (although as stated before the tools work best when integrated), the School Culture Survey is a good place to start. From there, the school—perhaps with the assistance of the school culture committee—can at least begin addressing the issues that need the most attention in the school. As stated before, the survey can help detect an early split between the staff and the administration and can occasion a discussion or dialogue on that issue before it becomes more difficult later on. The survey also can help identify a growing sense of faculty isolation, which school administrators can address more easily early on rather than later. On the other hand, the survey can also lead to staff members to celebrate the many positive aspects of their culture. This can generate positive energy to make an already good school even better.

- *What if the principal isn't on board?*

We have run into cases in which the principal was only partially on board and was not interested in having the staff take the School Culture Survey. Almost without exception, this proved to be a decision that the principal later regretted. At one school, the relations and trust level between staff and administration became so poor that the staff eventually signed a letter of grievances against the administration and hand-delivered it to the superintendent. Ironically, the district then requested that the staff take the very survey that the principal had rejected earlier. The problems are more severe now, and more energy will be required to rebuild trust than would have been if issues had surfaced six months earlier.

We initially designed the survey as a service to principals, having seen some blindsided by faculty tension they didn't know was there. It is also a tool for a principal (and the school as a whole) to track progress with their school culture. A principal might *feel* that things are improving, but a follow-up survey can provide data to help confirm this.

Therefore, as with teachers, we feel that appealing to what matters for principals—creating a school with a culture that elevates the performance and attitude of staff and students—can motivate them to take steps to more intentionally shape the school culture.

• *What if the touchstone grows stale and only a few teachers seem to be promoting it?*

Understandably, some staffs suffer from "mission statement fatigue." They may feel that the school touchstone is destined to meet the same fate as other mission-like statements at their school in the past and therefore not put much energy into promoting it. If the touchstone feels like a distant mission statement, then change it. It should feel vibrant and alive and inspire us to think and act our best.

We recommend reviewing all the suggestions in Chapter 1, but a few points are worth emphasizing. First, schools where the touchstone is most alive have developed structures to promote it. Typically students at these schools read the touchstone over the intercom daily or weekly as part of the morning announcements. This repetition helps create familiarity and comfort with the touchstone.

Second, asking students what they think of the touchstone can energize teachers. Understandably, teachers occasionally need reassurance that promoting the touchstone pays dividends whether in the hallway, during class meetings, or during literacy block. Consider surveying students about how, if at all, the touchstone is impacting them, and ask the staff the same question. Collecting such data might lead to tweaking either the touchstone itself or how the school promotes it, and it might lead to a reaffirmation of its value.

• *What if some staff members aren't convinced that the survey is really anonymous?*

Especially in schools with low levels of trust, some staff members need extra assurance that their responses are anonymous and cannot be traced. Though most of our surveys are taken online, we often provide paper copies to schools and allow staff members to place their responses inside a security envelope, which goes inside a larger manila envelope to ensure privacy. Some staff members, however, may remain unconvinced that their responses are truly anonymous no matter what steps are taken. There is little we can do about this.

We also have found that not all staff members have an e-mail address, and it is therefore difficult for them to complete the survey online. The paper surveys are especially important to ensure their input. (It should not be surprising that some of the most useful insights into a school's culture come from the paraprofessionals or even custodians who tend to see the school from a different vantage point.)

Those are some of the questions that we have heard asked about the process of using the tools from this book to shape a school's culture. Now let us turn to a brief summary of the tools and to a discussion of what they could look like when they fit together. Since a culture reflects a dominant mind-set, we have organized the discussion around each mind-set.

The school captures its core values in the touchstone; it expresses these values through its culture, which can be usefully separated into eight gateways. These values are most fully expressed when members operate from more highly integrated mind-sets as identified in the Four Mind-Set Model. The lessons learned from other settings and cultures can enhance the shaping of one's school culture.

Let's unpack what we mean by all of this. That the touchstone reflects the core values of a school community should by now be clear. It should also be clear that these values are expressed in its culture. Schools should identify key aspects of their culture and ask, "Do these reflect and support values in the touchstone?" Those that do should be embraced; those that do not should be reshaped or jettisoned. For instance, if your school values empathy, compassion, and critical thinking, yet operates a highly punitive disciplinary system that does not foster student thinking, then it should be reformed. If schools promote "love of learning," but the library is uninviting, the halls are absent of student work, worksheets are the dominant teaching tool, and external rewards and sanctions drive too much of the enthusiasm for learning, then something needs to change: either schools need to acknowledge they really aren't about "love of learning," or they need to reform their practices.

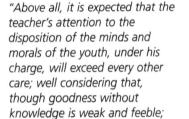

"Above all, it is expected that the teacher's attention to the disposition of the minds and morals of the youth, under his charge, will exceed every other care; well considering that, though goodness without knowledge is weak and feeble; yet knowledge without goodness is dangerous; and that both united form the noblest character, and lay the foundation of usefulness to mankind.
—Samuel Phillips, educator

The link between the eight gateways and the Four Mind-Set Model deserves more discussion. We contend that the school culture—entered into through the eight gateways—looks different and holds different possibilities depending on which mind-set you bring. A teacher operating from a mind-set of interdependence will approach a discussion of physical environment differently than one operating from a mind-set of independence. Those operating from the most integrated mind-set will see the fullest possibilities for each aspect of school culture. (Recall how dependence can be represented by a single line and integration by a large, three-dimensional box, reflecting the latter's more expansive perspective. See the first item in the Resources section of Chapter 2.)

Dependent School

Let's see how the eight gateways of a school operating from dependence (which we will refer to as a "dependent school") might differ from those of a school operating from independence, interdependence, or integration. At a dependent school, very few staff members take ownership of or clean the common physical space, leaving that job to the principal or custodian. The decorations in individual classrooms are sparse and largely functional. The rooms are pleasant but not inspiring. It is clear that teachers take little ownership for the physical environment of their classrooms—they have little sense that this is "my" space. The expectations passed down from either the administration or district are dutifully passed on to students without necessarily being adapted to their needs. At best, teachers pass on high expectations, but this depends on what comes from above. Teachers and staff dutifully, if perfunctorily, observe school rituals and traditions. However, they rarely initiate new rituals or suggest removing ineffective ones. The Founder's Day picnic goes on every year, even though no one, including the principal, knows much of anything about the life and virtues of the school's namesake.

As far as teaching and assessment are concerned, the teachers meet the guidelines set out by the district, but it is not clear that the teachers have internalized and taken ownership of these practices. The teachers teach the full 90 minutes of the literacy block and include its key aspects, such as a mini-lesson and silent reading, but they reveal little passion about what they are teaching.

Relationships at this dependent school are largely hierarchical, functional, and role-based. Teachers respect the chain of command and respect the position of the principal; however there is little sense of "we" here. Teachers do not pick up trash in the hallways, believing it the custodian's job; the staff rarely mix socially, and when they do they tend to stick to their own grade levels; sharp boundaries define the relationships between teachers and students, and you rarely observe much genuine warmth between them; some parents are involved but support only their children's classrooms. Relations in this school are clearly defined if not warm.

"The time spent on learning to care is not wasted; it is not time taken away from academic instruction. Kids who are friendly, happy, and cooperative tackle their academic work with more confidence, and both teachers and students enjoy greater success. They are not adversaries but partners in caring and learning."
—Nel Noddings, author (2002), p. 2

Predictably, students have little voice here. When teachers discussed enhancing student voice, they spoke mostly about setting up a student council to plan dances and fundraisers. The school's view of parent voice also had to do mostly with structures: is there a PTO and are we meeting its membership guidelines? Little thought is given to other dimensions of parental voice.

Likewise, leadership is seen in hierarchical terms. Increasing leadership for them might involve sending the principal and assistant principal to summer leadership training workshops but developing teachers and students as leaders is not on the radar screen here.

The school attempts to solve problems from a hierarchical framework as well. The principal tries to solve nearly everything alone including the latest issue: an increase in bullying behavior. The principal investigates various programs and, together with the counselor, selects one for the school and presents it to the staff—ostensibly for their input, but really to inform them of the decision. Most teachers are afraid to speak up at meetings and "rock the boat"; consequently key issues tend not to be addressed here or get swept under the table when they are brought up. For instance, the fact that boys' math performance in this school has been dramatically lower than girls' in recent years has never been addressed.

In general, a dependent school is characterized by a respect for hierarchy and authority. Things tend to run relatively smoothly, but there is little creativity, ownership, or even joy here.

Independent School

Compare this to what the eight gateways at an independent school might look like. At this school, teachers' classrooms are a natural expression of their personalities and their attitudes toward teaching. One immediately senses ownership in these rooms: a teacher teaching about rainforests puts fake trees in the classroom, including a stuffed gorilla hanging from the branches. In another classroom, posters of math work and math equations from students over many years fill the walls and reflect the teacher's enthusiasm for teaching math. In another classroom, the teacher has photos on the wall of every student she has ever taught.

For better or worse, teacher expectations similarly follow teacher tastes. Teachers in an independent school set their own targets and because they are committed and responsible teachers, they tend to meet them. These individual targets, however, are not aligned, and students experience gaps and overlaps as they progress through the system. Students benefit when these expectations are set high but lose out when they are low. For instance, partly because one elementary school teacher doesn't care much for math personally, math expectations are quite low in one classroom even though the teacher has exceedingly high expectations in other areas, including literacy, where the teacher is widely seen as an expert. Similarly, character expectations are idiosyncratic. In some classrooms, cheating is fairly common, as is talking back to the teacher; but to teachers in other classrooms, these behaviors are unacceptable. This ends up confusing students during their tenure at school.

"Effective character education is not adding a program or set of programs to a school. Rather it is a transformation of the culture and life of the school."
—Marvin Berkowitz, author (2002), p. 2

Teachers here observe school rituals and traditions, but they are prone to truly supporting only those to which they personally connect. One teacher, for instance, scarcely hides his displeasure—even to his students—at having to attend the monthly school assemblies, but he wholeheartedly promotes the annual student–faculty basketball game. At this school, new markers and rituals tend to develop from the passion of small groups of teachers and don't always involve the whole faculty. For instance, most of the staff are only vaguely aware that the fifth-grade teachers, both deeply concerned with social justice issues, join their students in the annual week-long "Write a Letter for Justice Campaign" sponsored by Amnesty International. They have been doing this for five years now, and younger students who learn about it are beginning to look forward to it. It is unfortunate, however, that this project isn't tied more tightly to work in other classrooms or to the school goals in general. There are probably a half-dozen small rituals like this in the school.

Some excellent teaching takes place here, but it is spotty. Since the teachers here are self-motivated, they seek out professional development opportunities and find other ways to improve their teaching. It is not uncommon for teachers here to be nominated (and sometimes win) state teaching awards. However, there are few norms here that would encourage the sharing of best practices. For instance, students in a few classrooms create rubrics for nearly every unit; in other classrooms students have never heard of rubrics. Perhaps more problematic is the lack of between-grade communication. A second-grade teacher tends to see students as "her" students instead of as future third and fourth graders. As a result, the teacher misses crucial opportunities to coordinate with those teachers on building important skills (such as writing and numeracy).

The quality of relationships is uneven. Teachers and staff tend to organize into cliques. These groups rarely mix socially or professionally and tend to represent voting blocks during staff meetings, which undermines the open and healthy discussion of new ideas. Because people tend to identify more with their group (often grade-level team) than with the school at large, it is difficult for whole-school initiatives to gain much traction. For instance, the whole school was to adopt the new antibullying program, but after a few months only the social worker and a few teachers still taught it. Teachers know each other's teaching by reputation, but very few have actually seen the other teach—even the one next door. To be fair, most people enjoy others on staff and enjoy working at the school; however, true collaboration is the exception more than the rule.

Relationships between staff and students are highly individualistic, and discipline styles vary greatly. Years ago the school tried to implement a schoolwide discipline policy, but those efforts quickly fell apart. Some teachers now use strategies from a "love and logic" seminar they attended last year. Some use very punitive strategies; one teacher notoriously yells at students (but no one has confronted him over this in the 11 years he has been at the school—teachers don't see it as their "business"). Most students feel they really connect with at least a couple of teachers, but the staff was surprised to learn that 38 percent of the students report not having a deep connection with any teacher. These students simply fall through the cracks.

In some classrooms, students enjoy a terrific amount of voice; even where little curricular choice is possible, they report feeling listened to by the teacher. But this emerges more out of individual teacher personality than out of a schoolwide shared agreement to honor voice. There are several teachers, for instance, who are very autocratic in the classroom and operate out of a "my way or the highway" mentality; but no one feels particularly justified in confronting these teachers. There are many afterschool student clubs for students to express their interests.

Teacher voice is uneven but strong. Many teachers feel comfortable talking and sharing at faculty meetings and approaching the principal with issues of concern. Some teachers, in fact, have too much voice and tend to bully others (especially the newer teachers) and even sometimes the principal.

This dynamic is also seen with parents. Parents are welcomed to be part of the school and serve on many of its committees. Some parents have even initiated their own committees. But parents tend to champion the interests of their own children instead of those of the entire school, and some parents simply have too much power.

Those who emerge as leaders tend to do so out of the force of their own personality instead of from any schoolwide, systematic attempt to nurture and distribute leadership. The same handful of teachers tend to be involved with the majority of the clubs and initiatives. While there is no schoolwide commitment to developing student leadership, many teachers do this anyway through a student council; but the degree depends on the particular advisor that year.

Issues arising at school are rarely faced collectively. This is not to mean that issues aren't dealt with effectively—they often are. However, many people feel out of the loop on issues, and the "lack of communication around here" is a common complaint. In some classes, teachers expect students to solve their own conflicts, but this is not the case in all classes. As is the case with many aspects of its culture, how problems are addressed—whether they affect the entire school, an individual classroom, or a single student— is a function of individual teacher personality instead of collective design.

The dominant quality in an independent school is individualism: teachers close their door and do their own thing. Teachers take responsibility and ownership for doing their jobs well but don't tap into or contribute to the collective talents of the staff. There are few shared agreements that hold the staff together and communicate its shared purpose.

Interdependent School

In contrast, most aspects of the school culture in an interdependent school result from collective design and shared responsibility. This is obvious in the physical environment of the school. Teachers here agree on the importance of physical space, therefore they take responsibility for their own room and the common space as well as the outdoor space. For instance, it took no time at all for the staff to tackle the graffiti problem—an obvious blight on the school. They decided that it was important for parents and visitors to feel welcomed, so they created an attractive space near the entrance with a table and coffee and cream. In addition, teachers take turns decorating the display cases each month with student work or something else relating to their course of study.

Academic and character expectations are universally high and aligned. This is partly because teachers spend time each week discussing student work and sharing best practices. In fact, all grade levels have created rubrics for what they call the "Five Agreements" that hold the school together. Therefore, there is no question about what type of teaching is expected or what constitutes high expectations. Since open communication is so prized here, teachers even have a protocol for bringing up issues with colleagues regarding the Five Agreements. For instance, a teacher recently shared a concern with a colleague whom she felt was allowing students to be disrespectful to him in class and in the hallways.

Except for rare cases, markers, rituals, and rites of passage here are collectively observed and supported. This is partly because the staff has weeded out those traditions that no longer have currency and have kept only those that do. For instance, the annual "Outstanding Student Award" speech no longer fits the character of the school. The faculty replaced this with a "wisdom speech" ritual in which each eighth grader passes on wisdom to the younger students in a five- to seven-minute speech. Supporting this ritual does not fall just on the eighth-grade teachers; even third-grade teachers reference these speeches and encourage their students to start thinking early about what they will pass on to others when they grow up. The school collects all the speeches on a DVD ("Wisdom of the Ages") and sells them at back-to-school night.

> "The evidence is now clear that strengthening sense of community promotes school bonding, and is central to students' healthy development—ethically, socially, emotionally, and academically."
> —Eric Schaps, author (2002)

Partly due to the Five Agreements—and the associated teacher-generated rubrics—teaching and assessment are remarkably consistent and of high quality here. Teachers are in and out of each other's classrooms all the time, and they meet weekly to discuss student work. This was part of their agreement to shape a Professional Learning Community (PLC) a few years ago. It is also a norm here to share best practices; teachers coming back from a conference, for instance, are expected to share highlights either with the entire faculty or with their learning team.

Teachers put a priority on creating caring relationships with students. In fact, this is one of the Five Agreements. Teachers individually greet students at the beginning of each class period, speak to them in a respectful tone of voice, and consciously affirm kids whenever possible instead of yelling at or humiliating them. Once a semester, the staff goes through a list of all students to identify those who might not have a significant relationship with any adult. Adults are then assigned to approach those students to try to initiate a deeper connection. This process has dramatically reduced the number of students who report feeling alienated and who might otherwise fall through the cracks.

Parents have been warmly invited to join in the "we" spirit of the school and serve in many volunteer roles, including on many committees. Parents have been encouraged to serve the interest of the whole school instead of just the interest of their particular children. Ironically, since this general philosophy has been embraced by the majority of parents, needs of individual children are better met now than before.

As with caring relationships, developing student voice is an explicit goal of this school that is shared by nearly all members of the staff. Therefore, the staff regularly discusses ways to monitor and improve student voice in the classroom and in the school as a whole. The school has an active youth council that works in partnership with the leadership team to improve things at school. For instance, the youth council recently shared concerns about the lunch schedule and is now working with the leadership team to arrive at a solution. Because students feel genuinely heard at this school, they approach the adults in a much more collaborative spirit than they might otherwise.

Teacher voice is also strong. Teachers feel comfortable approaching the administration with questions or concerns, and this is partly due to a schoolwide commitment to open communication. But what sets this school apart is not their willingness to voice new and creative solutions to problems but rather their willingness to support the group decision once it is made.

Leadership is widely distributed. The principal is in charge, but she has created an environment in which teachers, students, and even parents are involved in making decisions and are encouraged to provide leadership. This comes from a desire to tap into the collective wisdom of the school community.

Problems are almost always addressed collaboratively here. Staff members tend to support the final decision—even when they disagree with it—but at times feel bogged down in endless discussion and process. Some also detect a degree of groupthink and worry that innovative ideas don't always get their fair due. On the other hand, there is openness to addressing problems and a sense that things here are "healthy." For example the staff, led by the principal, created a task force to address the school's declining enrollment. There is no blame, just a willingness to confront reality.

The interdependent school is characterized by the honoring of shared agreements. What happens here is less a function of individual preference and more of collective design and agreement. The staff recognizes that the school can better meet the needs of kids when they support each other than when they go it alone.

A school that integrates the best from each of these mind-sets will be most effective at meeting the needs of its students. Such a school would have a proper respect for traditions and authority, take the benefits of individual teacher initiative, and support shared agreements toward a shared sense of purpose. Each member of the school—a teacher, student, parent, or principal—would appreciate the benefits (and drawbacks) of dependence, independence, and interdependence and would know which combination is appropriate in a given situation.

> "[I]f we recover a sense of the sacred, we will recover the humility that makes teaching and learning possible."
> —Parker Palmer, author (1999), p. 29

Closing

Over the past 30 years, organizations in many industries, from business to health care, have recognized the importance of creating a coherent organizational culture and have developed tools to build one. Increasingly, educators view their school culture as a resource as well: a healthier culture can translate into improved performance and well-being among students and staff, including increased academic achievement. Schools, however, have lagged other industries in building tools to effectively shape their cultures.

Our book is an attempt—imperfect, to be sure—to provide you with such tools. From our experience with more than 50 schools, we know that transforming a school culture is often difficult work. Results are rarely evident in the short-term. However, we have seen many successes. We have seen principals shift their leadership paradigm toward one that promotes collaboration. The staffs (including the principals themselves) are now reaping the benefits of working together instead of individually. Through the School Culture Survey, we have seen staffs show the courage to name the "nondiscussables" in their culture and take steps to address them. This has benefited both students and staff. We have seen schools bring new joy to teaching and learning once they clarified and affirmed their school's values, which they announce through their touchstone. We have seen schools creatively address seemingly persistent issues by using the eight gateways and by developing and holding to shared agreements, which have encouraged staffs to get on the same page.

A healthy school culture does not happen by accident: it is born from intentionality. We hope that the tools and stories shared in this book will help you take steps to improve that powerful and invisible force in your school: your school culture.

References

Atherton, J. S. (2005). *Teaching and learning: Groups: Dependence*. Retrieved May 25, 2007, from http://learningandteaching.info/teaching/groups_bad.htm

Barth, R. (2001). *Learning by heart*. San Francisco: Jossey-Bass.

Barth, R. (2002). The culture builder. *Educational Leadership, 59*(8), 6–11.

Bassett, P. (2005, March 16). Seven surprises for school leaders. *Education Week, 24*(27), 36–38.

Berger, R. (2003). *An ethic of excellence*. Portsmouth, NH: Heinemann.

Berger Kaye, C. (2004). *The complete guide to service learning*. Minneapolis, MN: Free Spirit Publishing.

Berkowitz, M. (2002). *Character education informational handbook and guide*. Raleigh, NC: North Carolina Department of Public Instruction.

Blankstein, A. (2004). *Failure is not an option*. Thousand Oaks, CA: Corwin Press.

Block, P. (2003). *The answer to how is yes: Acting on what matters*. San Francisco: Berrett-Koehler.

Bryk, A., & Schneider, B. (2002). *Trust in schools: A core resource for improvement*. New York: Russell Sage.

Bulach, C. R., & Malone, B. (1994). The relationship of school climate to the implementation of school reform. *ERS SPECTRUM: Journal of School Research and Information, 12*(4), 3–9.

Charney, R. S. (2002). *Teaching children to care: Classroom management for ethical and academic growth, K–8*. Greenfield, MA: Northeast Foundation for Children.

Collins, J., & Porras, J. (1994). *Built to last*. New York: HarperCollins.

Collins, J. (2001). *Good to great*. New York: HarperCollins.

Comer, J. (2004). *Leave no child behind: Preparing today's youth for tomorrow's world*. New Haven, CT: Yale University Press.

Crowell, S., Caine, R. N., & Caine, G. (1998). *The re-enchantment of learning*. Tucson, AZ: Zephyr Press.

Damon, W. (1995). *Greater expectations: Overcoming the culture of indulgence in our homes and schools*. New York: Free Press Books.

Damon, W. (2002, June 19). The roots of character and the role of community. Paper presented at the White House conference on character and community, Washington, DC.

Deal, T., & Peterson, K. (1999). *Shaping school culture: The heart of leadership*. San Francisco: Jossey-Bass.

Deal, T., & Peterson, K. (2002). *The shaping school culture fieldbook.* San Francisco: Jossey-Bass.

Edmonds, R. (1986). Characteristics of effective schools. In U. Neisser (Ed.), *The school achievement of minority children: New perspectives* (pp. 93–104). Hillsdale, NJ: Lawrence Erlbaum.

Eisler, R., & Miller, R. (2004). *Educating for a culture of peace.* Portsmouth, NH: Heinemann.

Elmore, R. (2000). *Building a new structure for school leadership.* Washington, DC: Albert Shanker Institute.

Enright, R. (2001). *Forgiveness is a choice.* Washington, DC: American Psychological Association.

Fullan, M. (1993). *Change forces: Probing the depths of educational reform.* London: Falmer Press.

Fullan, M. (2001). *Leading in a culture of change.* San Francisco: Jossey-Bass.

Fullan, M. (2005). *Leadership & sustainability: System thinkers in action.* Thousand Oaks, CA: Corwin Press.

Fullan, M., & Harvreaves, A. (1996). *What's worth fighting for in your school?* New York: Teacher's College Press.

Ginot, H. (1976). *Teacher and child.* New York: Macmillan.

Glazer, S. (Ed.). (1999). *The heart of learning: Spirituality and education.* New York: Penguin-Putnam.

Glenn, S., & Nelson, J. (2000). *Raising self-reliant children in a self-indulgent world: Seven building blocks for developing capable young people.* Roseville, CA: Prima.

Goleman, D. (1997). *Emotional intelligence.* New York: Bantam Books.

Gonder, P., & Hymes, D. (1994). *Improving school climate and culture.* Arlington, VA: American Association of School Administrators.

Houston, P. (1998). School reform or reform school? *Educational Leadership, 55*(5), 53.

Houston, P., & Sokolow, S. (2006). *The spiritual dimension of leadership: 8 key principles to leading more effectively,* Thousand Oaks, CA: Corwin Press.

Inger, M. (1993, December). Teacher collaboration in secondary schools. *CenterFocus.* Retrieved May 29, 2007, from National Center for Research in Vocational Education Web site: http://ncrve.berkeley.edu/CenterFocus/ CF2.html

Isaacs, W. (1999). *Dialogue and the art of thinking together.* New York: Currency.

Jackson, P., Boostrom, R., & Hansen, D. (1993). *The moral life of schools.* San Francisco: Jossey-Bass.

Kessler, R. (2000). *The soul of education: Helping students find connection, compassion, and character at school.* Alexandria, VA: Association for Supervision and Curriculum Development.

Kozol, J. (1991). *Savage inequalities: Children in America's schools.* New York: Crown.

Kruse, S., Seashore Louis, K., & Bryk, A. (1994). Building professional community in schools. *Issues in Restructuring Schools, 6,* 3–6.

LaFee, S. (2003). Professional learning communities: A story of five superintendents trying to transform the organizational culture. *School Administrator, 60*(5), 6–7.

Lancourt, J., Nevis, E., & Vassallo, H. (1996). *Intentional revolutions: A seven-point strategy for transforming organizations.* San Francisco: Jossey-Bass.

Lickona, T. (2004). *Character matters: How to help our children develop good judgment, integrity, and other essential virtues.* New York: Simon & Schuster.

Liker, J. (2004). *The Toyota way.* New York: McGraw-Hill.

Livsey, R., & Palmer, P. (1999). *The courage to teach: A guide for reflection and renewal.* San Francisco: Jossey-Bass.

Meade, M. (1993). *Men and the water of life: Initiation and the tempering of men.* New York: HarperCollins.

Meier, D. (2002). *In schools we trust.* Boston: Beacon Press.

Mid-continent Regional Educational Laboratory. (2004, February 9–10). *Balanced leadership: Leadership that works.* Workshop materials presented at McREL meeting, Denver, CO.

Noddings, N. (2002). Preface. In R. Charney, *Teaching children to care: Classroom management for academic and ethical growth, K–8* (p. 2). Greenfield, MA: Northeast Foundation for Children.

Noddings, N. (2003). *Caring: A feminine approach to ethics and moral education* (2nd ed.). Berkeley: University of California Press.

Noddings, N. (2003). *Happiness and education.* Cambridge, UK: Cambridge University Press.

North Carolina Department of Public Instruction. (2002). *Character education informational handbook and guide.* Raleigh, NC: Author.

Palmer, P. (1998). *The courage to teach: Exploring the inner landscape of a teacher's life.* San Francisco: Jossey-Bass.

Palmer, P. (1999). The grace of great things: Reclaiming the sacred in knowing, teaching, and earning. In S. Glazer (Ed.), *The heart of learning: Spirituality and education* (pp. 15–32). New York: Penguin-Putnam.

Palmer, P. (2004). *A hidden wholeness: The journey toward an undivided life.* San Francisco: Jossey-Bass.

Performance Learning Systems. (2004). Cooperative learning: Creating positive interdependence. *The Heart of Teaching, 83.* Retrieved May 29, 2007, from www .plsweb.com/resources/newsletters/hot_archives/83/interdependence

Peterson, K. (2002). Positive or negative. *Journal of Staff Development, 23*(3), 10–15.

Reeves D. (2007). How do you change school culture? *Educational Leadership 64*(4), 92–94.

Remen, R. N. (1999). Educating for mission, meaning, and compassion. In S. Glazer (Ed.), *The heart of learning: Spirituality and education* (pp. 33–49). New York: Penguin-Putnam.

Ritchhart, R. (2002). *Intellectual character: What it is, why it matters, and how to get it.* San Francisco: Jossey-Bass.

Rossi, R. J., & Stringfield, S. C. (1997). *Education reform and students at risk.* Washington, DC: Office of Educational Research and Improvement, U.S. Department of Education.

Sarason, S. B. (1996). *Revisiting "the culture of the school and the problem of change."* New York: Teachers College Press.

Schaps, E. (2000). Community in school: A key to violence prevention, character formation, and more. *Character Educator, 8*(2).

Schaps, E. (2002, June 19). Community in school: Central to character formation and more. Paper presented at the White House conference on character and community, Washington, DC.

Schlechty, P. C. (1997) *Inventing better schools.* San Francisco: Jossey-Bass.

Senge, P. (1990). *The fifth discipline.* London: Random House.

Senge, P., Cambron-McCabe, N., Dutton, J., Lucas, T., Smith, B., & Kleiner, A. (2000). *Schools that learn: A fifth discipline resource.* New York: Doubleday.

Sergiovanni, T. (1994). *Building community in schools.* San Francisco: Jossey-Bass.

Shein, E. (1992). *Organizational culture and leadership.* San Francisco: Jossey-Bass.

Steinberg, L. (1996). *Beyond the classroom: Why school reform has failed and what parents need to do.* New York: Simon & Schuster.

Thornburgh, N. (2006, May 29). Teaching doctors to care. *Time, 167*(22), 58–59.

Tomlinson, C. A. (2002). Invitations to learn. *Educational Leadership, 60*(1), 6–10.

Tucker, A., & Edmondson, A. (2003, Winter). Why hospitals don't learn from failures. *California Management Review, 45*(2), 55–72.

Walker, H., Ramsey, E., & Gresham, F. (2003). Heading off disruptive behavior: How early interventions can reduce defiant behaviors and win back teaching time. *American Educator, 26*(4), 6–45.

Wentzel, K. (1997). Student motivation in middle school: The role of perceived pedagogical caring. *Journal of Educational Psychology, 89*(3), 411–419.

Index

CORWIN PRESS

The Corwin Press logo—a raven striding across an open book—represents the union of courage and learning. Corwin Press is committed to improving education for all learners by publishing books and other professional development resources for those serving the field of PreK–12 education. By providing practical, hands-on materials, Corwin Press continues to carry out the promise of its motto: **"Helping Educators Do Their Work Better."**

Printed in the USA
CPSIA information can be obtained
at www.ICGtesting.com
JSHW062225270923
49290JS00009B/33

9 781412 953788